Journeying Home

Praise for *Journeying Home*

'After a century of hostility and competition between depth psychology and Christianity a new generation of psychotherapists are emerging who have learned the value of analytical techniques and understandings but can anchor them within the context of a mature understanding of the Christian vision of God. Fiona Gardner writes in a deceptively simple way, but this wise, sensitive and lucid book will be a treasury for clergy, psychotherapists, and most of all, everyone who seeks healing for life's hurts but hardly dares to hope that God cares for them.'

Chris MacKenna, St Marylebone Healing and Counselling Centre

'Wise, lucid and clear-sighted, Fiona Gardner proves herself a patient guide for troubled souls. As her clients struggle with thorny emotional dilemmas, she shows how the texts of our lives are reflected in the biblical narratives of old, and how psychotherapy and religion, after a century of mutual suspicion, can become allies on the journey towards spiritual truth.'

Howard Cooper

'The psyche, the field of dynamic psychology, and the soul, the field of spirituality, are no longer separate entities. They are intimately linked and any form of authentic prayer requires an understanding of both. This is precisely what this book achieves.'

Jack Dominian

'*Journeying Home* is a beautiful and courageous book. Fiona Gardner writes out of a deep spirituality and combines the experience and insights of therapeutic counselling with the journey towards God. Her accounts of the restoration of people with whom she has journeyed are both moving and life giving. Dropping her bucket into the deep wells of spirituality and therapy she draws from the wisdom of Merton and Jung as well as contemporary story tellers. The exercises and prayers with which the book concludes will make this a valued resource for many in today's confused and confusing world.'

Rt Rev. Peter Price, Bishop of Bath and Wells

Journeying Home

Unlocking the door to spiritual recovery

FIONA GARDNER

DARTON · LONGMAN + TODD

For Gemma and Dan with love

Published in 2004 by
Darton, Longman and Todd Ltd
1 Spencer Court
140–142 Wandsworth High Street
London SW18 4JJ

ISBN 0 232 52524 2

A catalogue record for this book is available from the British Library.

Designed by Sandie Boccacci
Phototypeset in 10.5/13.75pt Palatino by Intype Libra Ltd
Printed and bound in Great Britain by
Page Bros, Norwich, Norfolk

CONTENTS

ACKNOWLEDGEMENTS

➤✦

T HANK YOU TO Barbara Butler for her belief in me and my work throughout the 1980s and early 1990s. Thank you to all those people seen in my work as social worker and psychotherapist who have taught me to understand the depths of childhood despair.

I am very grateful to Prebendary Nicola Sullivan for her inspiration and ongoing help and support. Thank you also to the Revd Simon Airey, and the clergy and congregation of Bath Abbey.

I am grateful to all of the sisters of the Community of St Francis at Compton Durville for their kindness and hospitality.

I would like to thank Christine Stones who has read the book in draft form and been both helpful and supportive. Her comments about anger were especially insightful and have been included.

I would like to thank those other friends who have supported me in this new adventure, especially Gillian Bradshaw and Iris Tute for our regular discussions on spiritual matters over the years. Thank you to Peter Ellis for his helpful reflections on the text, and his love and support.

Thanks to Virginia Hearn and the staff at Darton, Longman and Todd who have shown me how it is possible both to be businesslike and to feel part of a shared enterprise. I have particularly welcomed Virginia's ideas and interest in the book.

Scripture quotations, unless otherwise noted, are from the

And Abram journeyed on by stages.

(Genesis 12:9)

The Christian gospel tells us not simply that we are saved from sin or that our guilt is taken away – it insists that we shall find out who we are and what we may be in an encounter, a relationship . . .

(Rowan Williams, 2000)

INTRODUCTION

✦

I REMEMBER THE INCIDENT so clearly. My friend and I were leaning out of our flat window early one Saturday evening. Down the road came fellow students whom we recognised as the 'God squad' excitedly on their way to a meeting. 'Look at them,' I sneered, 'how pathetic – who else would have them!' Then suddenly enraged by the sight of the group, I shouted, 'You bunch of losers!' I remember feeling rather pleased with myself, though slightly disconcerted when some of them waved smiling back at me.

What made me behave like that? Now I recognise only too well the longing to push onto others my fears and inadequacies. I can also understand my envious anger and false arrogance in the light of my own inner sense of loss, and in that way being 'a loser'. Underneath I felt unlovable and unloved, not sure where I belonged, and had to block out that realisation any way I could. Yet that group represented something that at some level I knew I needed and wanted, and about a decade later I began to search for it.

One of the things that I discovered was that my embryonic relationship with God repeatedly foundered on the basic issues of trust and faith. The past with all its difficulties and memories began to catch up with me and I needed help to sort out the worst of that. It was only then that I could begin to develop a full spiritual life less encumbered by blocks and obstacles.

The inward journey that I embarked on was both psychotherapeutic and religious. These are not the same and later in this book I think about the sameness and the differences, but

1

there is some overlap and certainly one can feed into and enrich the other. The book is partly about that overlap between religion and therapy, and about understanding what prevents us from loving ourselves and loving God. It is based on both my personal experience, and my professional experience as a psychoanalytic psychotherapist.

Religious people believe that life is about making some sort of journey. This sometimes becomes actualised as a pilgrimage, and for most of us it is a journey that happens internally and externally. What is that inward journey, and what does it mean for each of us? St Bernard of Clairvaux describes a process of change that happens within us, a journey from self-love to loving God. He perceives it as four stages of loving.[1]

> We love ourselves for ourselves.
> We love God for what he gives us.
> We love God for himself.
> We love ourselves for God's sake.

Such a traditional spiritual journey is seen to involve a gradual stripping away of what constitutes our outer self, our ego, the part that we present to the world. It would include all that falseness that bolstered me up in my attack on the Christian students. In that sense it is a dying to self and to all the desires and processes that uphold that false self. This false self is seen as self-serving, and it justifies an illusory state of autonomy and an illusory way of life. Dying to this self becomes possible through absorption with God, and so experiencing everything and everybody through the relationship with God, often understood through the person and example of Jesus Christ. For many this is an obscure ideal, and seems an almost impossible journey.

This book is an exploration of ways that might make this less obscure and more possible. It is about considering states of mind that are both largely before the start of St Bernard's stage one and almost completely rule out the second, third and fourth stages. It is about the difficulties some of us can have in feeling that we are at all lovable to ourselves, to others and ultimately to God. If there is a type of 'loving of self' taking place it may be a type contaminated by bad feelings, and merely an attachment to something familiar. Perhaps instead of loving ourselves we feel we 'hate ourselves for ourselves'. Such states of mind are characterised by restricted thinking, inhibited imagination, and a crippling expectation of what might lie ahead. This book is in part an exploration of a journey to recover an ability to feel love and compassion for oneself that can then allow the freedom of a true relationship with God.

Journeys usually start from a home of one sort or another. The inward journey that we embark on both in therapy and in our spiritual searching will probably start from the childhood home that we have lodged somewhere in our mind, even if it is somewhere we physically left many years ago. This may feel like a place we longed to leave, or a home to which we were and perhaps still are overly attached. Inevitably it will have included both good and bad experiences and have left us with various expectations for future relationships and our way in the world. It will also have left us with expectations that affect our spiritual life. The journey to understand this may take a winding and disconcerting route where we meet obstacles and worries we did not know lurked within us, but there will also be certain landmarks and satisfactions.

Where does this inward journeying take us and to what purpose? Most journeys take us out into the world and then we turn back towards home. The therapy journey certainly aims to take us out into the world, but perhaps it is left to the spiritual journey to find the turning within so that we can meet a part of ourselves which has never been away from our real home, and which welcomes us back to unity in the central and deepest part of our existence.

Who this book is for and how to use it

This book is a bit like a map to help guide us on the early stages of this inner journey. It is especially for those who feel they have lost their way, or who are exiled from the path, or who cannot get going – in terms of changing emotionally and spiritually. It is a book for all those who feel trapped by their past, and so separated from God. It is for those who feel that their relationship with God is distorted by expectations that originate from a difficult childhood. It is also for those who feel stuck and dissatisfied with their religious development.

If you are reading this book and working on your own you might find it helpful to keep a journal to record your feelings and memories about past events, and how they may be affecting you in the present. One idea would be to think of setting aside a regular time to work with each chapter, perhaps using a journal to write down memories and thoughts as they occur. It might be helpful to begin and end each personal session time with a period of prayer. A separate time for meditation can also be beneficial, as can relaxation and breathing techniques such as counting the breath, and following a rhythmic pattern of increasing and then decreasing breath lengths. Some ideas, exercises and prayers to use with personal session time are included at the end of the book.

It is also a book intended to be useful for those of us who have been in counselling or therapy, and who are looking for a way to integrate that experience with religious belief. Do the two experiences have to remain separate or is there a way of mutual understanding and enrichment?

This is also a book for all those working or training to work, whether in a pastoral context or a non-religious setting, with people who have experienced past trauma and pain, and who are seeking to recover their sense of well-being. Again the dynamics that might emerge in this relationship need to be respected. If we have had serious difficulties in the past we will bring, unconsciously, all our experiences from those relationships to any new one. In psychoanalytic psychotherapy this is called transference. Transference can become an opportunity to make real change, if we can realise that what we expect does not always need, or have to, happen. Similarly, if we are listening to another in distress it is inevitable that our own feelings both about the person we are listening to, and about our own experiences in comparison to theirs, arise. Sometimes these feelings can be surprisingly strong and powerful, and can even catch us unawares. This is called the countertransference. The feelings need to be internally noted, and if possible thought about later, rather than commented on or responded to at the time. It is important to try and distinguish between what is getting stirred up, and belongs to us, and the feelings that we may be picking up that belong with the person we are with. To make this distinction, we need to have a relatively clear sense of our own past with its difficulties and frustrations. It can often be helpful to talk these issues through with a third person, to clarify what is actually happening in the relationship.

This book is an invitation to make changes. It is an invitation to think again about our inward journey and the various aspects of how we relate to ourselves, to others and to God. It is an invitation to be open to ways of healing, and to make a choice between staying partly living in the past, or to be available more fully in the present. It is a journeying home.

Some background and definitions

Before setting out on a journey with someone it's useful to know a little bit about them and what they mean when they use certain words. The psychotherapy parts in the book are taken from my own personal experience as someone who was 'in therapy' over many years. I needed time to come to terms with my childhood and find ways of dealing with all the difficult and sad feelings I had about it. I had also developed a number of unhelpful ways of managing my relationships – as you can see from the incident at the start. When some of this was resolved I then went into training as a psychoanalytic psychotherapist, partly fuelled by the wish to give to others a similar healing and helpful experience. So, some of my professional experience is also included in the book. The 'psychoanalytic' tag means that I believe in the idea of an unconscious, and think about the conscious and unconscious dynamics that are involved in any relationship, including my relationship with God. As a child I went to Sunday school at a Congregational church, but lost interest as I grew older. As an adult for many years I was a Quaker, and also interested in the spirituality of yoga, and Buddhist meditation practice. However, I felt I needed something more defined, and something more personally involving as a relationship. After a period away from any formal religion I felt called to the Church of England and eventually became confirmed.

When I use the term 'religion' in the book it is as a broad concept denoting how a whole religious community lives with God. This includes its own teachings, sacraments, forms of worship, prayer and meditations, and the various forms of ritual. I use the word 'spirituality' rather more and with the particular meaning of a personal relationship with God as both transcendent and immanent, and through the person of Jesus Christ whom I experience partly as our bridge to God. This relationship may or may not be in the context of a particular church or branch of religion. Often 'spirituality' is used in a broad, loose way – in the 'I'm spiritual but not religious' mantra. This, as I explore later, usually avoids anything that requires or has implications for a personal relationship and commitment.

My interest throughout the book is in the personal, relational aspect of spiritual belief. At heart my belief is based on experience rather than doctrine, although I value liturgy and doctrine as providing a helpful framework for the relationship with God. My understanding includes consider- ation of God in the inner life of each person, and the way in which our attitudes, thoughts and feelings towards God are experienced and expressed in daily life and in our relation- ships. In other words the focus of this book is on the psychodynamics involved in the relationship with God, and the various ways in which, especially when affected by a traumatic past, they can act as obstacles to our life of faith and prayer, and an obstacle to the inward journey.

Our lives can be restricted and sometimes even blighted by a troubled childhood. What does that really mean? The first part of the map sets out an understanding of this and how we can be affected in all sorts of ways. The way the book then develops is in the form of a deepening journeying home through the use of three biblical stories. Each narrative pro- vides different and yet complementary routes that take us further into the body, mind and spirit dimensions in our inner journey. There are different stages of relief and recovery that take place as we gradually let go of embedded early experi- ences, and make space for something new and different. These are rather like signposts that mark the progress we are making.

> Build cairns to mark your way,
> set up signposts;
> make sure of the road,
> the path which you will tread.
>
> (Jeremiah 31:21 REB)

The three biblical stories set out the problem – or even the 'diagnosis' – which we think about in some detail in one chapter, and then the solution which we explore in the next chapter. The paths that we can trace through using these stories are already laid out for us and well trodden by others. Another story that gives us inspiration on our journey is that of the prodigal son. His route out into the world and then home to his father is thought about in each chapter.

What is it about childhood that makes our experiences so powerful? We need to explore this first and appreciate the search for meaning and order that we bring to trying to understand the past as part of our inner journey. Throughout we think about the implications for our potential or developing relationship with God.

CHAPTER ONE

✦✦

Making sense of our past

SARAH DESCRIBES a recurring dream. 'In the dream I am walking through a dense wood – almost a jungle with lots of branches and obstacles in my way – it's really hard work finding the path. As I come to the edge of the wood I find a beautiful coffin, it's made of dark wood with inlaid jewels. The lid is off and I can see inside, then I get really scared because it's completely empty. When I look up everything's gone and there's nothing in front of me – the wood's disappeared. It's like the universe is stretching on and on in front of me – but there's nothing in it.'

Sarah speaks of feeling that she is nothing – she looks all right, a bit like the beautiful coffin, but inside she feels empty. Things haven't worked out for her in the past and now in her thirties her marriage and her job are a mess – everything seems difficult and somehow gets complicated. She wants to make sense of it all – longs to find a meaning and a point to her life. 'I'm not a religious person,' she adds; 'I don't believe in some great powerful God, but it's funny, when I was a child I'd pray to God that I might leave home and that he could make everything all right.'

Dylan Thomas[1] wrote that the memories of childhood have no order and no end – this seems especially so of a childhood or adolescence that involved complications or serious difficulties. Often the memories are 'out of sequence' as the event or events have been impossible to understand and fit into a meaningful context, and therefore they remain unassimilated experiences – not fully known about but always there. Perhaps it feels as if there's a permanent black cloud framing the edge of our life. For example, imagine what it's like to experience continuous criticism and disapproval as a child – over time this becomes a fixture of our mental landscape. It means that still as an adult, the parent's or teacher's sarcastic or judgemental voice is present, especially when we are about to do something different or something that we are worried about, and so we feel a lack of confidence and anticipate failure. Perhaps we don't even bother to start. The childhood experience is still powerful and present as an internal voice in our mind.

What do I mean here by the phrase 'troubled' childhood and 'serious difficulties'? After all, inevitably we all have troubles in childhood – disappointments, feelings of rejection and disapproval, upsets, loss and separation. It is a normal part of growing up – it goes with the territory. However, for some of us as children these universal experiences can become cumulative, and so too much, or total in the sense of actually losing a parent through death or divorce, or being consistently unloved, and being consistently disapproved of. For others, this might include an abuse of power by the parent, such as serious neglect, or physical, emotional or sexual abuse, or a combination of trauma. When I use the expression 'a troubled childhood' in the book it is really to explain situations where there has been sustained damage, and adult life is affected. As one woman in her thirties told me, 'I had to grow up at the age of five – and it's all gone on ever since.'

There is often a reluctance to really think about childhood difficulties. Sometimes people say, 'I had a wonderful child-hood, I was very happy', but their expression, or the tone they adopt, suggests something different. Perhaps they are a bit too insistent about what fun it all was. Forgotten trauma and upset can emerge when something similar occurs in the present. For example, one man became filled with unreason-able anger when his small son tried to get his own way. The child refused to continue on a family walk and his father was infuriated. Later he recalled his own futile struggles with his father who could not be disobeyed. On the walk he had suddenly experienced the old fury he had felt as a child towards his own parents. This was combined in his adult role as father with his own father's belief that 'children shouldn't get away with anything', and 'being strict didn't do me any harm'. The inner conflict he experienced between the two positions of child and father led to the irruption of rage.

Even if we can remember, or half remember, childhood troubles we may prefer not to speak about them, or think it is wrong to dwell on the past. For some of us childhood can feel unbearable to think about, and so we go to great lengths to prevent memories from surfacing, or if they do we'd rather not talk about them. For others of us there's nothing to think about and the past doesn't feel relevant to the present. It may not always mean that we are preoccupied by the past, rather that it is repressed from conscious awareness. However, our old experiences – both good and bad – tend to emerge through our present relationships or our behaviour. We may not realise it, but often in our friendships we find ourselves attracted to people or to situations that repeat old patterns. For example, one woman who as a child took responsibility for keeping her mother well and happy found herself as an adult endlessly driven to make things all right for all those she met, especially older women, and at the expense of her own well-being.

For some people past pain feels ever present, and limits the sorts of relationships which are possible. The after-effects of a troubled childhood can be preoccupying, or catch us unawares. They can be upsetting, and confusing, and because of all this can affect us as adults physically, mentally and spiritually, and this we will explore as we journey on in the book.

If we return to Sarah's dream at the beginning of this chapter, it is possible that the dense wood – the jungle – that

Sarah dreams about, with its tangled branches and strange obstacles on the path, is representative of how she experiences her past and present life. She recognises that she is preoccupied with all that has gone wrong, and all that continues to go wrong. In fact she seems so caught up in it all, it's as if she cannot think straight, and has no emotional space left for any different experiences. She also suffers from aches and pains, and these leave her feeling low and anxious about her health. When we discuss the dream again, it almost seems that if Sarah did stop her preoccupation about the past there might not be anything to replace it – who would she be, and what would there be for her? If this identity dies she might be nothing, and it all feels very unsafe. Sarah speaks of longing for 'something bigger than me'. She says 'there has to be more than this', but there is no room for a relationship with God – only a long established hope for a God that can sort it all out – a good-parent God.

We are all wounded, we all know what it means to be vulnerable, to suffer, and feel pain. We also long for healing – for salvation. Some wounds cannot be healed in life, although easing of the pain can take place, and with it a measure of restoration. Sarah, though, is one of the 'talking wounded' – people who have recognised past pain, and the way they are caught in it, but who cannot find any way out from the mental maze. It feels like a half-alive state where the person is under siege to old patterns of behaviour and early experiences. Whatever is tried – new relationship, new job and new place to live – the past is still there, sometimes in a blatant way, more often in a subtle undermining manner. There is no freedom to develop in body, mind or spirit. Later on in adulthood it is impossible to find the 'truth' of what happened, and clearly not possible to change whatever the 'reality' was in childhood. Often very little is visible from the outside, the adult part continues coping but inside there is a different reality. Is it possible to lift the siege and feel fully alive in the present? Is it possible to start journeying home? How do we unlock the door?

Stages of relief and recovery

The journey of coming fully alive and achieving release from the past has four stages. When I first met Sarah she was *unconsciously preoccupied*. In other words she was not allowing herself to recognise what she was really feeling. She experienced physical pain and discomfort; in her thinking she anticipated downfall and disaster in everything that she undertook; and she did not believe that she could be genuinely loved and accepted. She knew that nothing felt right, and that a lot of the time she felt quite low. Her move to find someone to speak to followed a visit back to the area where she had lived as a child, where she felt so miserable that she knew she had to discover what was wrong with her.

As Sarah began to share her distress in regular sessions, she moved to a place of *conscious preoccupation* – in other words she began to recognise her physical, mental and spiritual distress. She was more in touch with the emptiness, and importantly she began to dream different dreams. This helped us start to understand her deep feelings, those that were especially hard to get in touch with. Gradually she became engaged in a process of change, and a small part of her began to trust me and the process of trying to make sense of her past.

The third stage was one of *consciously letting go*. This was a dynamic stage where Sarah gradually revealed her feelings of shame, guilt, anger and upset that originated from her past – a childhood that involved rejection by her father, who left when she was six with little further contact, denial of her identity as someone in her own right by her mother, and times of acute loneliness and loss. As she talked, Sarah realised the depth of her mixed feelings towards her parents, and realised how much the past patterns were casting a shadow on the present. Sarah anticipated that all relationships would turn out the same, and leapt on occasions when any semblance occurred. As we grew to understand the power of these projections, in other words the way she pushed onto others her experiences and belief that I or someone else would react in a certain way, it became possible to recognise them. These projections began to lose their power as she experienced a different outcome. Her usual way of thinking had been interrupted, and a new path involving change and the potential for love could be imagined.

The final stage was of *unconscious letting go*. Sarah did not have to think about what had happened to her as a child, and could live more fully in the present and get on with other things. Her imagination had become freer, she had faith in the possibility of successful relationships and that she could make her marriage work. She was able at last, if she wanted to, to believe in the possibility of a God who would accept her in all her complexity and confusion, and began to look for places to explore this embryonic faith without the restriction of past patterns.

Dividing the process of healing into these four stages is clearly an arbitrary progression. The stages are inevitably overlapping and interwoven, and there is always the possibility of a return to an earlier familiar state especially when under stress. However, I shall use this idea of the four stages as a way to think about change and transformation as part of each of the biblical stories used in this book.

There are also stages in our spiritual life and faith. The four stages of love described by St Bernard give us another framework. One of the ideas put forward in this book is that if part of us is restricted it may affect our belief in or relationship with the hidden God through Jesus Christ. It is as if the horizon of our knowledge about relationships then forms the framework of our reaction in our encounter with God. In other words our faith can get stuck in its development. So faith is not to be seen as just something that we either have or do not have, but as part of a developing relationship, an opening door, an extending horizon and a journeying home that can deepen as time passes and we change. The very earliest stage of faith involves trust and hope, and the book is mainly about exploring this.

Peculiar to childhood

How do we make sense of our past? Serious difficulties and troubles contribute to a shattering of our belief as a child that we live in a reliable enough and meaningfully ordered world. This is what we call a trauma. Just thinking about the word 'trauma' helps us understand the effect. Trauma is a wound – the term derived from the Greek, where it refers to a piercing and breaking of the skin. Therefore psychic trauma is the injury to our developing personality when sudden, intense and often unexpected anxiety overwhelms our ability to cope and defend ourselves from what is happening. Imagine the fear we might feel as an adult, suddenly surrounded by a group of aggressive drunk men who spill out of a pub we are passing. We are immediately aware that the situation could become out of control, that we are powerless as one against the group, that we might get hurt, and there is no one obvious to help rescue us. We are very alert, and feel frightened.

Serious childhood difficulties such as emotional, physical or sexual abuse, or loss and neglect, often take place in the home, and involve people who are significant and central to our life and on whom we depend. We can feel helpless and terrified, and our minds, and sometimes our bodies, can be flooded with a kind and degree of stimulation that is over-whelming. It feels as though something violent has happened inside, and this mirrors the actual events. Imagine you are away from home and suddenly think that you have lost your purse or wallet. Perhaps you panic, or perhaps you feel hot and cold. You might search in a hopeless or increasingly frantic way – all sensible thinking has gone and you start to imagine the worst. Perhaps you are irritated or angry. It is only gradually that you find a way to manage the situation and it preoccupies you until it is resolved. Multiply the effect a hundred times or so and we have a sense of the panic, fear and disorder that we feel as children if our sense of equilibrium is knocked.

In other situations the drip-drip of small but repeated experiences, such as continuous criticism or anxiety about a parent, become overwhelming. This involves a slower but no less powerful disintegration of our fragile mental structure. We can get a sense of this if we think of regularly having to meet someone who we know doesn't like us or who is imposs-ible to please. We start to dread the encounter – perhaps we steel ourselves to face them, or find ways to avoid meeting them. We develop a headache before we see them – then it's easier not to go. It has all become too much. Again hugely multiply the feelings and we glimpse the state that we might experience as children dealing with a disapproving parent.

One fourteen-year-old with a disruptive and abusive childhood wrote this poem:

Thunder quakes,
I stand alone,
my body shakes,
without a home,
I cradle a haunted soul,
locked within,
an everlasting hole.

A child cries,
blinded by tears,
tries to scream,
but no one hears,
locked in my mind,
the prison gates too high,

she tries to find,
the reasons why.

The emotional shattering from the impact of serious child-hood difficulties is the breaking up of the expectations of the established way of going about one's life, and beliefs about the predictability of the world. As can be imagined, the younger we are when these experiences happen to us, the less well we are able to cope. If we are neglected or abused from infancy then we are never able to establish beliefs and a sense of predictability, other than those based on what we have known. We can either only repeat that with others or turn our unhappiness on ourselves.

While reactions may appear later, at the time of the events we might just go on behaving almost as usual, even if we are falling apart inside. This is the terrible feeling that the adult spends his or her life trying to avoid, whatever the cost.

V. S. Naipaul, the novelist, gives us a sense of this. In a 1981 interview he said:

'I have two very early memories of my father being mentally ill and of waking up in a hospital room and being strapped in a bed. Pneumonia my mother tells me. But I have always been fighting a hysteria that plagued me as a child.'

'What activates it?'

'The old fear of extinction and I don't mean dying. I mean the fear of being reduced to nothing, of being crushed.'

Here V. S. Naipaul describes an ongoing effect of trauma. The terrible fear of being 'reduced to nothing' is a good description of being psychologically overwhelmed, a state of fear that no one would want to re-experience. His childhood re-emerges in his fiction, where every so often the reader glimpses V. S. Naipaul's early experiences. In *The Enigma of Arrival* he writes, 'To see the possibility, the certainty, of ruin, even at the moment of creation, it was my temperament', and later in the same book, 'the fear of extinction which I had developed as a child ... the fear of being swallowed up or extinguished ...'[2]

How can we trust the adults around us, or even trust anyone, when those whom we respected and believed in have let us down and betrayed us? This loss of trust is what becomes lodged in our minds as the black cloud at the edge of our life, and it usually includes feelings of helplessness, inadequacy and guilt.

George Orwell was sent away to boarding school aged eight, and writes as an adult about his memories of being beaten by the headmaster after wetting the bed: 'He had a habit of continuing his lecture while he flogged you, and I remember the words, "you dir-ty lit-tle boy" keeping time with the blows.' Then the beating was repeated:

> This time Sim laid on in real earnest. He continued for a length of time that frightened and astonished me – about five minutes, it seemed – ending up by breaking the riding crop. The bone handle went flying across the room.
>
> 'Look what you've made me do!' he said furiously, holding up the broken riding crop ... The second beating had not hurt very much either. Fright and shame had anaesthetised me. I was crying partly because I felt this was expected of me, partly from genuine repentance, but partly also because of a deeper grief peculiar to childhood ... a sense of desolate loneliness and helplessness, of being locked up not only in a hostile world but in a world of good and evil where the rules were such that it was actually not possible for me to keep them ... I had a conviction of sin and folly and weakness, such as I do not remember to have felt before ... I accepted the broken riding crop as my own crime. *I* had broken it: so Sim told me, and so I believed. This acceptance of guilt lay unnoticed in my memory for twenty or thirty years.[3]

In his discussion of the link between George Orwell's childhood and his books, Leonard Shengold[4] comments on the characteristic (in George Orwell's description of the broken riding crop), that if we are wronged as children we still take on the guilt that the self-righteous adult so often lacks. Why does this happen? As children we often feel responsible, bad and guilt-ridden almost on behalf of the adult. For example, most young children usually feel that if a parent is sad, or angry, or even ill, it must be something that they – the child – have done. This is all the more powerful if the child is also being hurt. This false sense of responsibility can lead to feeling very anxious around the parents or adult. After all, what might happen next?

For many people who have not had such experiences, this taking on of the responsibility and the guilt for what has been done by the adult may feel hard to accept. Yet it is an experience known by many. A combination of anger, upset, fear and love for the adult involved, puts us in a contradictory mess. It is this that leaves us bearing the outcome for the terrible events of childhood which then has lasting repercussions for later adult life.

The experience with the adult who hurts us either emotionally, or physically, can get right inside us in the sense that our personality and very being is altered, body and soul. One woman said, 'My mother always told me how much she liked this girl down the road who was everything I wasn't, and how awful I was compared to her. I remember trying to be more and more like this girl, but it didn't work – my mother still said she didn't like me.' It is the ability to feel for oneself that is fundamentally altered. This is where we can stumble at St Bernard's first stage of loving. How can we love ourselves if we feel responsible for feeling bad? How can we be lovable if it is our fault that the adult upsets or harms us, or doesn't like us?

If our trust is broken then we have little confidence, low self-esteem, and strong feelings of inadequacy – 'I'm not good-enough' and 'I'm bad' can dominate our thinking. Our relationships with others are affected, and we may seek out people who remind us of the adult who upset us, partly because that's what feels normal and right. It all becomes so horribly familiar.

Sometimes angry emotions can come to dominate but the form that these take is usually not straightforward. The anger can remain inside us, leading to an extreme of passivity and victimisation. This can also lead to attacking our own body and self. One way is to sabotage every new venture, which then confirms the feelings of being 'no good'. Another is to turn to behaviour such as harming ourselves, or abusing food, drugs or alcohol. Alternatively as adults we can identify with the powerful adult who hurt us, like the father with the small boy on the family walk, and in turn re-enact the awful experiences on someone else – perhaps our own child, or partner. Another option is to move from self-destruction to wild rage, leaving others fearful of our emotional un-predictability and mood swings. Others of us can be left feeling frozen, in a state of numbness, and terrified by anger, and any expression of feelings. We run from any glimpse of conflict or disagreement. Whatever our reaction, we are drawn away from the fullness of life, back towards the shadows of the black cloud and the compulsion to repeat past experiences in every new venture.

Relating to God

If Christian spirituality is about a relationship with a personal God who loves us and who can only be encountered person-ally, then all the dynamics, commitments and risks associated with relating to other people are also involved in our relation-ship with him. Perhaps there is not even the remote possibility that there could be a God to whom we could hope or dare to relate: 'I feel so bad and worthless – why would God want someone like me?' How can we imagine that we are loved by God when we don't even like ourselves?

Such wholehearted rejection of a personal God is a huge defence against the potential of a good experience, or the existence of a good and benign relationship. After all, if such a possibility is allowed then the person risks immense feelings of grief, loss and deep longings, as they well up from the past. How can *we* accept who we really are, full of fear and anger and sadness – let alone God? In contrast, some spiritual practices such as yoga or meditation are sometimes seen as offering a safe space for impersonal emotional sustenance, a point I shall return to talk about further in the book.

There are different reasons why we turn away from the idea of a loving God; sometimes it seems especially at the point when we most need to find and be found by him. My understanding is that sadly at the point where we are broken, and hopeless, we can become shut off and closed to any spiritual comfort. We might be angry, injured or defeated. This is why I find myself using words such as 'besieged' and 'preoccupied'. We are told in Psalm 51 that God does not despise a 'broken and contrite heart', and can read of Jesus' acceptance of the outcast, the rejected and the mentally and physically ill, but if we are unconsciously preoccupied in the way that Sarah was, in the way of the adolescent who wrote the poem, as V. S. Naipaul speaks in the interview and writes in his books, and as George Orwell writes in his novels and essays about the past, we cannot hear these words, let alone allow ourselves to experience them purely and without our own soured prejudice. Our embryonic relationship with God, and the first steps of our journey to love, can become distorted and contaminated by our past. The door stays locked.

God can take on the attributes of the all-powerful tormentor who punishes at will. Through such distortion and the projection of our expectations, we come to expect a critical, punishing, vengeful God. Then our relationship becomes a bit similar to placating an unpredictable and difficult parent. Guilt can become the cornerstone of our religion, with self-punishment the means of control. Perhaps in the past we desperately needed to keep the parent good, whatever had happened, and this led to keeping the bad feelings inside. The resulting distorted split (distorted, in the sense that it comes from an unhealthy part of our thinking) is that the parent (God) is right and good, while we as the child (now adult) are all wrong and all bad. This needs to remain rigidly in place and under our adult control, in case the old pain emerges and knocks us off balance again.

This leaves room neither for the development of love nor for a true sense of forgiveness. We cannot 'love ourselves for ourselves', and it is impossible to 'love God for what he gives us' except in a masochistic and distorted way. Although in such a state of belief God is seen as 'all good', it is the result of traumatised thinking, so it is in the old form – the old split – and in that sense is a denial of a truly accepting and loving God. Such religious belief is operating at a very primitive level. In some ways it links to magic thinking – 'if I do this then God won't let that happen' – and fits with an early stage of our development, when if we were very quiet and good we might escape further trouble or pain.

Another variation is the idea that God is only interested in our very good – our falsely good – self. This then denies all the mess and disorder from the past. No matter how much the past feelings arise, they are crushed down with an inner severity that merely repeats the earlier experiences. We cannot be loved for who we are; we are reduced to nothing – extinguished for the benefit of God. In fact the benefit is secretly of and for us, and so remains false.

Often being very good around God is also a way of denying our terribly angry feelings. This may be anger towards God who allowed our suffering, and an avoidance of thinking about the implications of God's anger. How can our past experiences be reconciled with a loving God: 'A loving God – you must be joking after the life I've had!' 'How could he exist and allow my misery?' Some people speak of their anger towards God – 'if there is one'. As shown in my embarrassing outburst against the students, Christians are often the butt of aggression and derision. They are ridiculed or dismissed as irrelevant by those who are most threatened by the idea of God, and the implications of the vulnerable, crucified and suffering Christ.

There are problems posed by all suffering, perhaps especially that inflicted on vulnerable children, in our understanding of a loving God. How can God have created a world that allows such horrors? Is God angry with us? Yet coming to terms with suffering and being angry with God is potentially part of our relationship with him. Anger can be a block on the development of our faith, but if we allow ourselves to acknowledge our anger our faith is freed, and we can experience God alongside us in our pain. It can be seen as a creative and hopeful action, signalling a restoration of feeling and faith. Expressing our anger, rather as some of the writers of the psalms do, is something we return to later in the book.

Sometimes, however, we cannot afford to have any feelings about anything, let alone anger. Parents or carers may have squashed any emotion from an early age. Perhaps as children, like Sarah, we were not allowed to mention the existence of the absent father, let alone any feelings about being left. Sometimes we have to stop all our feelings in order to look after our parent, who demands all the emotional space. If feelings become detached or even dissociated – in that neither events nor associated feelings are remembered – then a relationship with God may follow a habitual but totally non-reflective path. This is a form of psychic numbing. In other words, to have real feelings about God, or really to commit to Jesus Christ, is too dangerous: emotions may become overwhelming, or feel out of control, so we merely go through the religious motions. God is felt to be far away and needs to be kept in that position at all costs. In this state, God is also put in the position of being detached, calm and undemanding, unconnected to emotion and pain.

Finding a route out

Somewhere in our mind we attempt to make sense of things – as in the poem by the adolescent, 'She tries to find, the reasons why'. Making some sense of what has happened helps us, and makes the mess feel more manageable. Starting to try to make sense is like looking on the map to find the way before we start a journey. The map is only two-dimensional and looking at a map can never substitute for the actual travel, but it can help as a rough guide. We need to find a route out that offers a different experience and new opportunities.

If body, mind and spirit are all adversely affected by past difficulties, then restoration work has to be attempted in all three, although inevitably all three are closely interwoven. In this book we move to think about the nature of the after-effects, how we feel physically, how we think, and the way we develop spiritually. There are paths of healing on this journeying home shown through the stories described. On the route are landmarks of relief and recovery with the signposts leading us through unconscious preoccupation to conscious preoccupation, and from conscious letting go to unconscious letting go. Here are the movement and the stages needed for transformation to occur.

The search to unlock the door and find the route out and to feel better urges us on as adults as it once led us to discover and find things out as small children; it is part of the human condition. We want to feel restored; even if we put down those who try to help us, there is a part that longs to become healed and whole. It is this search that may lead some people to seek help. The need is for an opportunity to speak about what is happening and what has happened in a safe place, where there are also clear structures as to the nature of the relationship. We need to be heard so that we have a sense of who we are.

We need to perceive that the other understands, and

empathises with our story. For all those who listen there is a desire to understand and meet the person in a helpful way. There can also be an associated anxiety to have to come up with meanings and solutions. This can become a cul-de-sac and a way of avoiding our own helplessness as we hear about unhappiness. We may long to make everything better or to cover distress with platitudes, but the task is to uncover, open up and be alongside the person as they acknowledge their vulnerability, rage and pain. Whether we embark on this journey of love alone or with another person we can find well-worn paths in biblical narratives that help us in our self-reflection and self-discovery.

Biblical guidance

In the Bible we have accounts of trauma and suffering, and we also have accounts of healing – often over generations. The inherited wisdom contained in such stories frequently includes both the diagnosis – what is wrong with the way things are – and the prescription for salvation. The narratives are also descriptions of how intimately God is involved in human life, even when we have turned away and refuse to acknowledge him.

Howard Cooper talks about the Bible as an adventure in mythopoetic storytelling – it is a form of narrative. He goes on to write of 'this ancient tradition of storytelling as the medium for exploring truths in symbolical and metaphorical forms'.[5] The Bible offers ways of thinking and perceiving experience, and narratives that we can, in our individual responses, learn from.

Often we see in the Bible narrative different accounts of the same events. The four gospel accounts of Jesus' life and death testify to that. Through differing perspectives we can see shades of meaning and states of indeterminacy. We also all have our different understandings of the stories that we read and the way that we respond to them. Other options become possible; so there becomes room for thought and discussion, and personal variations in faith. The Bible narratives teach us to embrace uncertainty and what is not yet known, and to live with what may be possible. They help us to use our imaginations, perhaps putting our own experiences into the stories and thinking through how we might have responded in similar situations. They can also give us inspiration and consolation.

Thinking about unfinished business from one's own past is in part about crafting a new narrative. The idea is that the previous preoccupation with the set and stuck story gradually becomes replaced by a different angle and perspective. Already what felt hardened and set in concrete has begun to be loosened up into probability and possibility. There will also be stories about what it feels like talking to someone new or writing our journal or starting to pray and talk to God. Another layer lies in the connection between the past and the present: is talking to God or the priest beginning to feel like talking to a parent? If so, can it be thought about and interrupted?

There are three well-known 'macro-stories at the heart of Scripture'. Marcus Borg suggests that these three stories image the religious life in a particular way.[6] I am taking these stories and exploring them in the context of healing and unlocking the door to spiritual recovery. They can help us in the stages of our journeying home. The first is the story of the person who feels shame and guilt and seeks forgiveness. We may feel bad because of actual wrongdoing but, as with George Orwell and the broken riding crop, as children we more often take responsibility for the adult's wrongdoing. The second is the story of oppression and then the exodus from Egypt. The third is the story of exile and return from Babylon. Each story offers us guidance, a bit like a map, on our route out from our troubled childhood. Clearly the three intersect, but each has a different resonance for those coming to terms with a troubled past. Each is a process and a movement from stasis to change. In the course of the book the three stories will provide a framework for thinking about the state of preoccupation and the restoration and transformation that can follow in our journeying home.

Two travelling companions accompany us on our way and we will meet them now.

Alan's story

When Alan and I first met he told me that he was thirty and depressed; sometimes he had panic attacks, which left him feeling anxious. He worked in a residential home for people with severe learning difficulties, and had a long-standing girlfriend, who was very supportive, and they planned to marry.

Alan was the younger of two brothers; his father had sometimes worked away from home during Alan's childhood. When he was eighteen months old, his mother became physically ill and family friends looked after Alan, while his brother stayed with the father. After three months Alan went back home, but his mother was repeatedly ill during his childhood with periods away in hospital. As a child Alan remembered feeling anxious, and had trouble getting to school, often complaining of feeling sick. At secondary school things went better and Alan remembered enjoying time with friends.

The two brothers had gone to a Sunday school run by the Methodists, but he felt this was to give his mother a break and he stopped going at thirteen. Alan told me that as a little boy he had worried about hearing that Jesus could see whatever you were doing. Now he didn't know what he thought or believed, but a couple of times when he felt very low he had gone into the large church in town which was often open, just to sit.

Kirsty's story

Our other fellow traveller is Kirsty, who was forty and worked part-time as a school dinner lady when we met. She had one daughter, nearly grown up, and felt very protective of her. She was divorced from her husband who, in her words, had been a bully. Kirsty felt very badly about herself and her past. As a young woman she had cut herself, and taken several overdoses; now she sometimes drank too much. Kirsty said she wanted to understand why she felt as terrible as she did – there must be a reason.

Kirsty didn't remember much about her childhood. She was more concerned about what people thought about her, and whether they judged that she was as terrible as she felt herself to be. When I asked about religion, Kirsty laughed in a dismissive way – 'Why would God want to know someone like me? I feel bad through and through.' She had been to church services with the school – Christmas and leaving cere-monies – but added, 'Anyway, what church would have me now?'

In the next chapter we pick up the first path on our journeying home based on the biblical narrative of shame, guilt and forgiveness, and so together with Alan and Kirsty – let's go!

CHAPTER TWO

Feeling ashamed and guilty

IT'S HARD TO REACH St Bernard's first stage of love where we 'love ourselves for ourselves' if we feel ashamed and guilty. One difference between the shame and guilt we feel as a child and that we feel as adults is that usually as a child the wrongdoing is not our fault. Yet although as children we might have been the recipients of the wrongdoing, nonetheless we often carry the feelings of guilt and responsibility that really belong with the person who wronged us.

How do we find our way out of this maze of self-recrimination? This chapter explores the first part of the route: reflecting on our feelings of shame and guilt. The second half of the path is about the 'solution' of acceptance and forgiveness, and this is explored in Chapter 3. In both chapters we use the New Testament story of the adult Peter's betrayal of Jesus and his later forgiveness. What do we do with our guilty and shameful feelings? Sometimes they can deeply affect the way we see ourselves. Can the story of Adam and Eve also help in understanding the process? Perhaps we are unconsciously preoccupied with these feelings and need to move to the stage of conscious preoccupation, so that at least we are aware of our distress. What are the implications of this? Any such preoccupation seriously restricts or distorts our potential relationship with God, and this is discussed. In this chapter we start to get a better sense of the difficulties experienced by Alan and Kirsty, and also look at the first part of the well-known story of the prodigal son.

Peter's story – the betrayal

In both the Old Testament and the New Testament there are many accounts and references to this sequence of guilt and forgiveness – it seems one fairly constant way of thinking about the religious life. In the Hebrew Scriptures the sequence of sin, guilt, sacrifice and forgiveness is often linked to an institution of ancient Israel, 'namely, the temple, priesthood, and sacrifice. Within this story, the priest is the one who makes us right with God by offering sacrifice on our behalf.'[1] In this Old Testament model we become people who have disobeyed and broken God's laws, and who then stand guilty before him. The priest will intervene on our behalf to lessen our punishment from God. In other words we need to pay penance for our wrongdoing, and hope that this will undo what we have done. In the New Testament the death of Jesus is seen as the sacrifice for sin that allows God to accept and forgive us, and so Christian liturgy emphasises the sequence of confession of sins and absolution.

One of the most powerful New Testament stories is that of Peter's betrayal of Jesus when Jesus is arrested. Perhaps we can identify with both Peter, who betrays, and Jesus who is betrayed, abused and abandoned. Clearly this is an account of the relationship between two adult men, but perhaps we can relate this too to our childhood experiences of being wronged, and see how this leads to the adoption of the burden of guilt.

In the account of Peter's relationship with Christ, we see someone who loves Christ and promises to stand by him no matter what happens, but who is then caught in a world of harrowing experience. Following Jesus at a distance, and yet so closely, Peter demonstrates his hope and bravery, his fear and cowardice, his grief, his love and his misery. He denies that he knows Jesus three times. When he recognises this betrayal – the cock crows twice, and he remembers how it was foretold and how firmly he had rejected that possibility –

'he broke down and wept' (Mark 14:53–54, 66–72). In this passage we can empathise with Peter, and imagine the fear, sorrow, shame and guilt he felt when he realised what he had done. The part of the story that links so powerfully to the context of childhood shame and guilt is the shattering of the relationship, the idea of betrayal, and all the associated feelings.

We can also perhaps identify with Jesus, who is betrayed and carries the guilt of those who reject and abuse him. He is left alone and silent in the place of shame – so like the experience of the betrayed child. For as children we are naturally loyal to our parents and caregivers. It is all that we know, and we usually have to accept what happens. When we are betrayed the relationship is shattered, but we often remain loyal, carrying the bad feelings for the adult, rather than acknowledging our mixed feelings. Often it is crucial for our sense of identity that we keep the parent as 'good', and so the 'bad' feelings become stuck inside us, just as we are often stuck in the 'bad' situation. As described in the previous chapter, there can also be a mess of contradictory feelings involved, such as anger, fear and upset. The powerful feelings and the strength of our outrage can sometimes leave us feeling guilty. Peter was open with what he felt, but as children, we often have to hide our feelings, or are not allowed to express them. The betrayal by the adult becomes our betrayal and their guilt our guilt.

Imagine what it feels like to long to see the father who moved out of the family home. Imagine waiting at the window for a sight of him, with the gradual realisation as the hours pass that he is not coming to visit. How easy to feel that we must explain away his absence, excuse him or even blame ourselves for his not wanting to come. At all costs we need as children to keep our parents as good and on our side, even if we betray and wrong ourselves in the effort. We need to love them and hope to be loved by them. In the Bible story we understand why Peter felt terrible, and how he carried those feelings until his guilt was forgiven. We also have a sense of Jesus' desolation and grief.

The story of guilt and forgiveness as part of the journey home

Unlike Jesus and Peter, many of us find it hard to turn to God for consolation in our distress. Why can't 'we love ourselves for ourselves' and 'love God for what he gives us'? If we are besieged by fear, guilt and shame about what has happened in childhood, we feel so bad that we cannot be forgiven, cannot forgive those who inflicted the pain, and cannot forgive ourselves. There is a resonance with this experience aside from any connection with Christianity. It is a sequence that in part already makes sense, especially to children. What do I mean by that? Children usually feel that things are their fault: if mummy is sad, or daddy leaves, or their parents are rowing or cross, children often feel responsible even if what is happening is nothing to do with them. If the child is part of what has happened then the worry, anger and guilt about it feels even stronger.

Sometimes, as is explored in Alan and Kirsty's experiences, the feelings are repressed, and we certainly don't think about them, but they re-emerge years later through the body either in physical symptoms, or in the person's body image, and the way they treat and respond to their body. It is, in a sense, then a distorted form of self-love, or rather self-absorption, that rules out a genuine sense of relief, compassion, recovery and forgiveness. St Bernard's words about self-love, 'We love ourselves for ourselves', are not really relevant in the way that I think he implies. Instead there is something more like dislike and disrespect for the self, and this can sometimes lead to self-punishment, which is often inflicted on the body perhaps through too much drink, or too much food, or not enough food, or hurting ourselves in some way. Any self-love that is present is in a terribly distorted form, and follows a distorted sequence. In this way we do wrong to our own self and to our body as a result of the wrong done to us.

For some of us hurt in the past, a mental sequence gets established of fear, shame, guilt and sacrificial self-punishment in a misguided attempt to achieve some form of release. This is a pattern without the relief of acceptance and forgiveness, and without the intervention of a loving God. It can become stuck and a very familiar way of being. This is shown in the next instalment of Alan's story below, where he became his own judge and lawgiver with a system of strict requirements and sacrifices.

Yet perhaps there is the possibility that the sequence of shame, fear, guilt and self-punishment could lead to a different outcome and the way into faith. Perhaps this could become the starting place for recognition of the past; and a changing of the experience of being wronged and wrongdoing, of guilt and self-punishment, through the relief of God's acceptance and forgiveness. Perhaps we could even feel compassion for ourselves?

Thomas Merton, the Catholic monk, whose experiences I shall draw upon in different parts of the book, remembers as a child struggling with his experience of his mother as, 'worried, precise, quick, critical of me, her son'. Yet he found it troubling that in contrast others spoke of her as, 'gay and light-hearted', and of her 'happy laughter'. How do we as children deal with such a disjunction? Once again there is the tendency to blame oneself. Thomas Merton confirms his feelings of responsibility for his mother's apparent change in character, which foreshadows his repressed sense of responsibility for her later illness and death when he was only six years old. He reflects on her 'insatiable dreams', and 'great ambition after perfection'. He continues, 'Maybe that is why I remember her as mostly worried: since the imperfection of myself, her first son, had been a great deception ... I was nobody's dream-child.'[2]

It's a short step in the mind of the child from not being

good enough in the parent's eyes, which leads to the parent being worried, to feeling shame and guilt for being 'bad' and 'destructive'. This sense of shame and guilt can feed on itself, and this seems to be confirmed when Thomas Merton writes of 'the devils that hung like vampires on my soul' that his baptism failed to loose. Compounded by the trauma of his mother's death, issues around shame and guilt accompanied Thomas Merton for many years, and affected both his sense of self and his relations with others – especially with women.[3] This raises the obvious concern that if shame and guilt go unacknowledged, and are kept right out of our conscious awareness, they will become part of the black cloud that is always with us. Not only is our bodily behaviour affected, but also our future relationships with others, and then inevitably with God. It is also clear that later experiences can compound the earlier ones, thus confirming the sense of shame and guilt.

The first story of shame and guilt

Shame and guilt seem part of the human condition and for many of us can act as an internal judge and jury. The capacity to feel guilt is what assures us of our recognition of doing wrong, and often in the mind of the child reveals the experience of being wronged and sinned against. In childhood it usually links to a failure in being loved, perhaps through neglect, intrusive parental behaviour, or actual abuse of some sort. The sense of guilt is sometimes conscious and if that is the case it is clearly declared. People suffering from severe depression, for example, often express morbid guilt feelings about what they feel or think they have done. Even if the instances they are speaking about seem trivial, the impact in the mind of the person can be very powerful, and reassurance makes no difference.

In contrast, an unconscious, repressed sense of guilt can explain unusual behaviour or somatic problems. In other words the guilt links back to something that happened many years before, which has been pushed down and is no longer in the forefront of our mind, but is still affecting the way we are and how we behave. Perhaps we have never previously thought about this sense of guilt, but if we dare to uncover the feelings it might help us to find what our behaviour really means.

Shame also can last a long time, as it is our own self-image that we have injured. By violating how we like to see ourselves we can become lost to ourselves. Loss of self-respect and the failure of liking ourselves can feel unbearably painful. Fear is linked to both shame and guilt. We can be frightened by what has happened to us, and by our feelings towards the people who hurt us, but also we can be frightened by our shame and frightened by the prospect of punishment for our guilt. We can also be ashamed of our fear, especially if the person who has hurt us is a parent, or someone we are supposed to love.

When we feel ashamed we want to disappear – we can hardly bear to see ourselves or to be seen by another. We stand humiliated, 'shamefaced', and long to vanish: 'I wanted to sink through the floor' or 'crawl into a hole'. The last thing we want to do when we feel ashamed is to think and reflect on it.

In an early Bible story, we read about the creation of Adam and Eve, and their expulsion from the Garden of Eden. This account documents the first sin, which leads to the discomfiting states of shame and guilt. The move from Paradise and separation from God is accompanied by these very emotions. The misuse of freedom through the act of disobedience, and the desire for what was forbidden, led to guilt at the action, and shame at the knowledge and exposure of what had happened. Adam and Eve hear God, who calls out to Adam 'Where are you?' In response Adam says 'I heard the sound of you in the garden, and I was afraid, because I was naked; and I hid myself' (Genesis 3:10). Here is fear, guilt, exposure and shame – and the response is to try to hide – both body and self. These are all states that we have to confront in our own lives if we are to allow ourselves to have a relationship with God. 'Then the eyes of both were opened, and they knew that they were naked; and they sewed fig leaves together and made loincloths for themselves' (Genesis 3:7). Thomas Merton understands this scene as 'the first step in that self-alienation which resulted from man's refusal to accept himself as he actually is'.[4]

We need to try and accept who we are, and what has happened to us, no matter how badly we feel about it, no matter how great the shame and guilt, no matter how strong the fear, and no matter whether we feel it our fault or realise that the adult concerned is to blame. This is the only route out of a stuck state. Taking a first step in acknowledging what has happened to us will help us start to know ourselves, and may in turn offer us the choice and opportunity to start to know God.

As children, we often have to accept situations over which we had little, if any, control. This is even more frightening and hard to think about. In Maya Angelou's autobiographical novel she describes what it feels like to be an abused child – to feel helpless, inadequate and guilty in a world one never made. She writes, 'A textured guilt was my familiar, my bedmate to whom I had turned my back. My daily companion whose hand I would not hold.'[5] Maya Angelou is describing the weight of guilt and fear following her experience of child sexual abuse, and the subsequent murder of the rapist by enraged family members. Her sacrifice, and self-inflicted punishment, was to remain silent, believing that her words when she spoke about what had happened then contained the power to kill. She attempted to turn her back on the ever-present guilt. Many children remain silent through shame and guilt, but are still, even as adults, in some way punishing themselves. Some may feel ashamed of their feelings and thoughts; others feel guilt about what has happened to them.

As silence falls so the shameful and guilty feelings remain and the punishments and sacrifice grow heavier as the child grows older.

Alan – unconscious and conscious preoccupation with shame and guilt

Alan told me that when he went into the church in town to sit, he had tried to pray to God. He sometimes felt so desperate that he could not think where else to turn. He asked God to save him especially when he was feeling very anxious and panicky. Sometimes inexplicable aches and pains in his body brought on his panic attacks. If the pains lasted for longer than a few hours, Alan would be convinced that he had something terribly wrong – perhaps terminal. He would search his body for lumps and distortions, with his heart beating loudly, full of fear at what he might find. As he worried more so it sometimes seemed the pains increased until eventually something else diverted him, and he would note later, with surprise, that the pain had gone. If nothing diverted him Alan remained anxious, ruminating on the grey future ahead, until the aches eased and exhaustion set in. His girlfriend was supportive, but concerned about Alan's miserable state.

He told me that sometimes he would strike a bargain with God. If Alan was very good and did an extra piece of work for a colleague or volunteered for an extra shift – especially when he did not want to – then he hoped that God would spare him from an early death. So far that had worked, though Alan found himself setting increasingly high stakes in the form of doing more and more as penance. He didn't understand why he felt ill all the time. At one point he had gone for a check-up with the doctor, but had felt so worried by how seriously she took his complaints he could not face returning. So far all tests had been negative but just suppose there really was something the matter – how could he cope?

37

Alan was preoccupied both with his health, and his need to placate an increasingly powerful and vengeful God. Alan's God demanded many sacrifices, but why did Alan need to be doubly punished – both through the body pains, and then through the extra 'good' work to make sure that he did not die? Over time, in therapy, we worked out together from everything that he told me, that Alan needed God to see that Alan was very good because of all that he did, so as to avoid God seeing that inside Alan felt very bad. Our therapeutic task was to try and unravel what was going on in Alan's mind, and what was causing all the aches and pains. The location of the body symptoms often provided a clue for us – a pain in the neck, terrible aches around his shoulders, sudden sharp pains in his bottom and stomach, ear ache and head pains. It seemed worthwhile to try and read the body symp- toms – what was he trying to communicate in his distress? Who was felt to be a pain in the neck and in the butt? What burden was he carrying on his back? What did he not want to hear or think about, and could not digest?

It emerged that a great deal of the anxiety about illness belonged back in his childhood, when Alan had become increasingly worried about his mother's physical and emotional health. She had seemed so tired and withdrawn, and complained about all she had to do. He had thought he was responsible, and if he was very good that might prevent her illnesses. That seemed a clear link, but at another level Alan was taking on the illnesses, not just to save his mother along the lines of 'if I become ill then she will be all right', but also as a way of punishing himself for all the mixed feelings he had towards her. The real fear belonged back in the time when family friends looked after him when his mother was in hospital. The feelings evoked by the early separation, when he was eighteen months old, were still very active in his unconscious, and involved the fear that he might be destructive, and have caused his mother's illness. This is because he had felt both fear and anger about his early abandonment by her. As she had been ill, and he had to be a good boy when his mother was better, these feelings were repressed, and Alan felt both shame and guilt about what he had felt, even though the memory of the actual feelings had long disappeared from conscious awareness. His aches and pains were a form of self-punishment for his 'sins'. He looked a good boy, always helpful towards mummy, but he knew and so did God that inside he felt very different. This was the dynamic that Alan projected onto God and that formed the basis for his relationship with him.

As Alan began to understand that the aches and pains might be psychological, and so therefore have a different sort of meaning, he was able to feel less frightened. He could recognise that he was preoccupied by unresolved feelings of shame and guilt from his past that had got lodged in his body in the form of symptoms, and that these had affected how he was thinking (or not-thinking as it turned out), and how he was imaging God. As he began to feel less anxious, and felt that I could tolerate and think with him, Alan could start to speak more freely about all the longings and loss of his childhood, and his resentment towards his parents for what had happened.

The function of witnessing

Alan was caught in a complex and, for him, a familiar place. He was really stuck in a place of shame and guilt. He firmly believed in punishment and retribution, but alone had found it difficult to disentangle the causes of his shame and guilt. He needed to feel able to understand the predicament of how he had felt as a very small child, and that what had happened to his mother had not been his fault. However, the present feelings that he carried from the past experiences were his responsibility, and it was these he had to share and talk about, and open up, before he could take the second part of the route out from this stuck place.

39

By speaking to someone, childhood difficulties and troubles can become known and heard. What was stuck as a private preoccupation is given a public voice, and something begins to change. A door begins to open. A different form of witnessing takes place through composing poetry or writing a journal. If we write about what has happened to us as a story, or in our diary, or in a poem, or try and draw or paint scenes from childhood, we start to open up both ourselves and the past. This begins the move from a state of unconscious preoccupation to conscious preoccupation and our gradual realisation about our past.

The teenage girl, whom I shall call Sophie, whose poem I quoted in the last chapter, wrote about some of her experiences. She wrote about her lost childhood and told me in therapy that as she did, the past became more real than the present. Sophie had been plagued by flashbacks, sudden and unwanted images of some of the awful things that had happened to her when she was about eight. She wrote about feeling 'stained with impurities casting loss and shame' upon her. When she finally and bravely wrote about the images in her mind they seemed to stop haunting and attacking her. The past gradually became more under her control and somehow contained by the words on the page.

We see the functioning of written witness in the Bible stories. Not only are the events recorded for future generations, and there is inspiration for others to follow, but also through this act of witnessing we see the presence of God alongside the struggles and hardship.

Kirsty needed her story, which is described next, to be witnessed – in this case it was in the presence of another person – by someone who did not know her or her family, but who offered a listening sanctuary where she would not be judged.

Kirsty – unconscious and conscious preoccupation with shame and guilt

Kirsty told me that she felt unworthy of being loved by anyone – least of all by herself. She could scarcely think about herself, so desperate was she to blot out her feelings. She did feel loved by her daughter, but dismissed this as 'the poor girl has no choice but to love her mother'. Kirsty had no emotional room to think about self-acceptance, as she was preoccupied, and besieged, by states of shame, guilt and low self-worth. She did not at first realise this but gradually, over time, began to understand the weight of her predicament. In other words her unconscious preoccupation moved to a state of conscious preoccupation.

When we first met, Kirsty found it hard to look directly at me. She had cut her hair so that it fell forward over part of her face, and she sat hunched over, so that the shape of her body was indistinct. She seemed anxious not to expose herself to me – perhaps I would see something that she wanted to hide, perhaps something that she needed to keep under control. Everything needed to be concealed. She often brought heavy bags of shopping with her to our meetings – she was literally as well as metaphorically weighed down by baggage.

After a while Kirsty told me that she was frightened about what I might think about her family – how I would then judge her. At one level it hadn't been a bad family, but she knew now that it could have been different. As she slowly talked about them, a picture emerged of her family life, characterised by her father who drank heavily and who was strict, aggressive and bullying towards his wife and children. Her father had been in the army and the family had moved every few years, which meant Kirsty had never really settled in school or made lasting friends. Her mother had found looking after the children difficult, and Kirsty had felt singled out at some of the schools she had gone to because she had not had the right uniform, and her clothes were often rather worn. A couple of times she had been bullied and picked on at school so had tended to 'bunk off' and miss lessons. She had left without any qualifications, so felt stupid, and had tended to find casual work until she became a school dinner lady at a local primary school, which she enjoyed, mainly because of the friends she had made. Both parents had died in the previous year, and it seemed that this, plus her concern about her drinking habits, had prompted Kirsty to seek help.

When Kirsty described her family, she would sometimes quickly look up at me. She wanted to check my face for signs of disapproval and disgust, and it became clear that Kirsty herself felt embarrassed by what she told me, and expected censure and disapproval from me. Kirsty felt shame by association with her family and their behaviour. She also felt ashamed about her self and her own behaviour. Kirsty felt worried and shameful about how she was seen – how she looked, and the way she sometimes behaved, especially when she drank too much. She saw herself as 'yuk', 'all horrible inside', and no matter how clean she kept herself and her house, a feeling of being stained seemed to permeate her experience.

As we slowly got to know her story, it seemed that part of the feeling of being contaminated was linked to unacknowledged anger and rage towards her father. He had on several occasions behaved in a violent way towards Kirsty and her brothers, and the children had all, at various times, witnessed frightening scenes of domestic violence. These experiences had led her to intense feelings of confusion, so much so that she had begun to doubt all her memories, including the marital violence that she had witnessed. She remembered thinking as a child that perhaps it was all happening to another girl. At one level, even as an adult, Kirsty had partially maintained this way of thinking in that, although she had never forgotten that she also was the other little girl, she also had never wanted to acknowledge how awful her childhood had been. As she began to reflect on her troubled childhood she experienced mixed feelings. Behind the shame and the guilt she realised that she had felt very frightened of her father, and now as an adult understood how in her terror she had had to cut part of herself off and become the child who denied that anything awful was happening.

The violent family life had left Kirsty with layers of feelings of guilt – as Maya Angelou describes it, 'textured guilt'. The feeling that she was to blame for the state of the family and her father's violence towards her mother preoccupied Kirsty. As a child she had witnessed her father's moods and aggression, and thought that, as she was part of it, it must somehow be her fault. She berated herself with why she hadn't been able to stop her father hitting her mother. She felt responsible and therefore guilty. She also remembered feeling both fear and excitement by his attention, and now remembered with horror her feelings of power when as a teenager she wore provocative clothing and felt his eyes on her body. Perhaps she had colluded in something terribly shameful. If she had then her body had betrayed her and colluded with the bully – her hateful father. Hurting and punishing her body had been a way of dealing with all the contradictions involved.

As Kirsty began to speak about her childhood she found that she was consciously preoccupied with remembering and trying to make sense of what had happened to her and what had gone on in the family. At this time Kirsty needed consistent support and time to think about what she was feeling. As she acknowledged the extent of her father's violence, she was able to link this to her feelings of contamination, and the emerging feelings of shame and guilt. She understood why she had needed to cut and harm herself as a young woman, and more recently why she had begun to drink so heavily – anything rather than cope with thinking about what it had all been like. In her move from unconscious preoccupation to conscious preoccupation, Kirsty had become aware of how much she was suffering. She also understood why she felt guilty and so ashamed of herself and her family. When an adult betrays our trust as children, we are thrown into a state of shame resulting from the loss of our most profound attachments. In order to keep the adult as 'good', we judge ourselves as 'bad' and fall speedily into a state of guilt.

Critics of talking cures such as counselling or therapy might suggest that things are best left in the past but, as I hope is becoming clear, if we leave the past as unfinished business we are not free to live our lives to the full. Some Christians may feel that everything needs to be left to the grace of God, but again, as I think is shown, without some comprehension, and reconciliation of our inner turmoil, we are restricted at all levels of our being – perhaps especially so in our capacity to develop a true relationship with a God who can heal us and help us to receive from him.

The prodigal child

The prodigal son is an especially powerful story for those who are coming to terms with a troubled childhood, and one that I return to think about in each chapter. By changing 'son' to 'child' the story becomes more inclusive and clearly available to both men and women. The story acts as a template for all three ways of healing. This wonderful story told by Jesus is primarily a story of sin, shame, guilt and forgiveness; yet it is also a story of oppression and liberation from restrictive and unhelpful thinking to new possibilities, as well as a story of self-alienation, exile and homecoming to belief. It is a timeless narrative for us all – both sons and daughters.

The story arises in the context of those who are lost and then found: 'there is joy in the presence of the angels of God over one sinner who repents' (Luke 15:10). Both Alan and Kirsty were lost in their past difficulties. Neither had followed the literal example of the son in the story and squandered money on good times. Both had been wronged as children, and were not responsible for the behaviour of their parents, but both carried the 'sin' and the feelings associated with it. However, like the prodigal son, yet in a metaphorical sense, both were wasting their lives in a cycle of grief, shame, guilt and recrimination. In that sense the spiritual legacy was caught up and wasted in a place of wrongdoing, and being wronged. 'Sin' separated them from the chance of relating to God. Such preoccupations were an obstacle to a relationship with God, and a rejection of what was being offered. Yet both Alan and Kirsty longed for an experience of being loved and accepted.

Henri Nouwen, in his rich exploration of this story, reminds the reader of the radical implications of the son's leaving. It is both a heartless rejection of the home, and a break with tradition. Implicit in the actions of the son is 'Father, I cannot wait for you to die.' In other words there are murderous feelings involved. Henri Nouwen carries on to explore this part of the story metaphorically as 'a denial of the spiritual reality that I belong to God with every part of my being, that God holds me safe in an eternal embrace, that I am indeed carved in the palms of God's hands and hidden in their shadows'.[6]

Alongside the spiritual rejection involved in states of shame and guilt, is (as already explored) the idea of self-punishment. Punishment such as savage and sudden death, or banishment to hell, is often associated with religion. Jesus' ministry takes place against a backdrop of punishment as implicitly linked to illness or disability, though Jesus also refutes this. The 'punishments' experienced by Kirsty and Alan, and so many who have had difficult childhoods, are forms of self-punishment. When wrong things happen there is not just a loss of love involved but also strong feelings of rage and hate. What can we do with these angry and aggressive feelings? If they cannot be expressed against the people who have hurt us then they are turned inwards against ourselves, and we can end up treating our bodies as worthy of chastisement.

We can beat ourselves up by hurting or abusing our bodies in different ways in an act of repentant self-punishment.

The hatred and anger is about murderous rage. Hell is present and happening now! Alan saw his symptoms as leading to an early death. Kirsty had experimented with risk-taking behaviour such as self-harm and heavy drinking. Anger turned against the self implies angry murderous feelings towards another that have been diverted. How can we find a loving spiritual home when we realise that we feel so angry? We are ashamed of feeling such passionate depths of anger, especially in a Christian context where love and peace is emphasised. There is often a longing to fit in with what is associated with 'being a Christian', and anger and outrage don't seem readily to belong. There can be an anxiety about being found out or found wanting. There can be huge anger towards God for allowing what happened in childhood. These worries can prevent and certainly distort any relationship with God. We need to find our way towards God, and can sometimes do this through the person of Jesus Christ. In this relationship we need to be able both to seek comfort and to expose the angry, upset feelings. Then there is the chance of forgiveness and guidance, as in the story of the prodigal child.

In Milton's *Paradise Lost*, Lucifer says,

> So farewell hope, and with hope farewell fear,
> Farewell remorse: all good to me is lost;
> Evil be thou my good.[7]

The poet expresses how shameful and guilty feelings can only be experienced with the revival of hope and aspirations about good relationships. In other words, included in the besieged, stuck, preoccupied state of self-hate are the seeds for change and movement to love. There is present within the anxiety and depression a possibility and a potential for feeling better. In the next chapter this potential is explored through the movement towards acceptance and forgiveness.

CHAPTER THREE

Movement to acceptance and forgiveness

Hᴏᴡ ᴄᴀɴ ᴡᴇ ᴍᴏᴠᴇ ғʀᴏᴍ these desperate feelings of guilt and shame to feeling better? If the last chapter contained the diagnosis of what was wrong then this chapter explores the necessary prescription – acceptance and forgiveness. This is a huge step on our journeying home. Once again here is the paradox of which we need reminding: that our bad feelings stem from what has been done to us, not what we have done to another; but it seems that it is ourselves that we have to accept and forgive. Can the Bible help us here?

The story that we began to look at in the last chapter was Peter's and his shame and guilt at having betrayed Jesus. Peter is accepted and forgiven for his betrayal in the wonderful story of Jesus' appearance to the disciples on the lake shore. What joy to realise that the person you felt you had destroyed and let down by your actions is there waiting to welcome, forgive and feed you. In John 21, we read of Peter's forgiveness by Jesus. Jesus cancels out the pain and guilt of each of the three betrayals and affirms his relationship with Peter through love and nourishment. The process is utterly cleansing, and gives us a glimpse of the trust that can be felt in relationship. In his eagerness to meet again with Jesus, and repair the past, Peter turns towards Jesus and jumps into the lake to swim to the shore. Here there are earlier echoes of the story of Peter testing his faith and trust in Jesus by walking on the water and in doubt starting to sink (Matthew 14:22–33). That story took place in the evening amid the storm and wind; the forgiveness takes place in the clear light of the morning with a breakfast celebration. Peter is now well acquainted with his own darkness and more realistic about the depths of faith and sustenance needed. He is ready to be forgiven.

There also may be resonance for us in the story of the paralysed man whose friends lower him through the roof for healing by Jesus (Mark 2:1–12). Jesus commends the men for their faith and heals the man by saying that his sins are forgiven. The connection between sin and sickness was commonly assumed – though Jesus warns against it (Luke 13:1–5 and John 9:3). The ensuing debate with the scribes, usually understood as being about honour and authority, may also contain useful psychological insight. Perhaps Jesus understands that the paralysed man feels so bad about what has happened to him it is easier for him to hear he is forgiven and so recover, than to be told to get up and walk. Perhaps it is easier for us to recover from our paralysed, stuck state of fear and shame if we can feel forgiveness, rather than just being encouraged to get on with it and walk away from our past. Another process needs to happen before we can do that.

In God's promise of restoration for Israel and Judah, the prophet Jeremiah bears witness, and we read, 'Your hurt is incurable, your wound is grievous . . . your guilt is great', but despite this pain, change is possible: 'I will restore health to you, and your wounds I will heal' (Jeremiah 30:12b, 15b, 17). Guilt does not always have to lead to punishment: it can lead to recovery through forgiveness. The phrase 'turn again and be forgiven' (Mark 4:12) is used interchangeably with 'turn and be healed' (Isaiah 6:10). If we can forgive and be forgiven, we can be healed. In the process of healing we find ourselves discovering forgiveness and compassion.

The language used in Judaeo-Christian religion of 'sin', 'evil' and 'atonement for sins', and so on, seems hard to accept, especially in the context of unhappy and upsetting childhood experiences. Such language raises worrying questions. When children are abused is that a sin, or evil? Is it more of a sin if the abuse is sexual rather than emotional? When ill mothers neglect babies is that a sin? Is it more of a sin if they are alcoholic, or drug addicts? Is it a sin if mothers live their lives through their children, and only love them if the child does what the mother needs and wants? Is divorce a sin, or parents who quarrel? Is it an equal sin if they stay together and barely speak? The difficulty is that the more we know the more complex are the issues. Many who ill-treat others have been ill-treated as children. Many brought up in violence only know that way of expressing themselves. Many intrusive parents are deprived of their own sense of identity. Many parents are somewhere still needy unloved children, and know no other way of getting these needs met. Is such lack of love between generations a sin or evil? And who are we to judge?

In the story of Adam and Eve the man and woman are little more than small children, they are innocent, and do not know what they are doing by their action. Through their separation from God by their act of disobedience they start to recognise difference – between themselves and between them and God – and the idealised state of fusion and harmony is lost. Was Eve's action sinful enough to justify the long history of the church's attitude to women? As we understand more, so we realise that our behaviour as humans is often complex, and less easy to define as sin, or good or bad.

Perhaps we can understand sin better as that which pre-occupies us, makes us feel miserable, and contributes to our self-absorption and separation from any possible relationship with God. Surely it is about our blindness and our wounds, and our state of captivity. It is about all these feelings and states of mind and behaviours that prevent us from loving God and one another. We cannot be responsible for our upbringing, but we can begin to take responsibility for how we feel, how we respond to one another as adults, and how we treat our own children. None of us are in such isolated circumstances that we cannot begin to see that other ways of living are possible, even if only gleaned from television or exposure to other families. Yet in our contemporary society so many people feel guilty and shameful, as though they are in some way unacceptable and not lovable.

For anything to be different, we need to be able to turn or change our position and the perspective in which we see ourselves and what has happened to us. There is, I think, also a close relationship between forgiveness and awareness, knowing what we are doing, and being able to think about what we feel and how we behave, and this will be discussed further in subsequent chapters.

Forgiveness involves making a choice and making a change. In Philip Roth's novel *The Human Stain* a young man, Mark, breaks down completely following his father's sudden death from a car crash. 'Mark Silk apparently had imagined that he was going to have his father around to hate forever. To hate and hate and hate and hate, and then perhaps, in his own good time, after the scenes of accusation had reached their crescendo and he had flogged Coleman [his father] to within an inch of his life with his knot of filial grievance, to forgive.'[1]

The choice is whether to change and find a way out of our preoccupations with the past into a state of letting go. Only when we let go of the past can we be fully involved in the present and plan for the future. This poem extract puts it succinctly:

> a voice speaks from far South Africa
> of reconciliation and
> puts a definition on forgiveness:
> 'It is' the bishop says,
> 'a way of dealing with the past
> so as to plan the future'[2]

In terms of the stages of relief and recovery outlined in

Chapter 1, forgiveness involves conscious letting go, which will in time lead to unconscious letting go through a gradual easing of tension towards another person and towards oneself. In this chapter we explore this process both from the perspective of forgiveness as a Christian ethic and from the psychoanalytic perspective.

What is forgiveness?

This is a difficult word to define partly because it is complex: there are many layers and aspects to it. As with our consideration of guilt, 'forgiveness' has a textured quality. Rather like the word 'love' it also has a quality that is hard to grasp, something mysterious and elusive, with, as we know, an aspect of the transcendent to it. Unlike shame it is not a universal experience – something in the nature of how we are; instead it seems to be something we can receive or obtain, and something we can in turn experience towards others.

Theologically, forgiveness cannot be understood outside of the framework of God's forgiveness, or without reference to those emotive words 'sin' and 'evil'. Sin is often linked to not putting God first, worshipping other gods or idols, or to self-importance and putting affairs of state before acknowledgement of God. In the Old Testament the idea is linked to the idea of atonement, often in connection with sacrifices that are then made. Another interpretation involves the idea of sin being lifted and taken away. Forgiveness, then, is part of the nature of a gracious God: 'you are a God ready to forgive, gracious and merciful' (Nehemiah 9:17b), and 'there is forgiveness with you' (Psalm 130:4), are two examples of Old Testament witness. On the human side there is an implicit need for penitence before we are forgiven.

In the New Testament there are different words used in the translations, and these can open up how we think about forgiveness. One means to deal graciously with, and another to send away and to loose, another to release. In the Lord's

51

Prayer we understand that if we are forgiven we must in turn forgive – and this needs to be a genuine act. Jesus' teachings demonstrate that human and divine forgiveness are closely linked, although presumably one is a poor imitation of the other. Forgiveness in the New Testament is closely linked to Christ himself, arising from all that he is and all that he does. Most powerfully the connection is made with his death and resurrection. Our experience of Christ frees us to see properly, heal our wounds and unlock our prison gates. We are encouraged that through faith and repentance we can reach a place of forgiveness: 'If we confess our sins, he who is faithful and just will forgive us our sins and cleanse us from all unrighteousness'(1 John 1:9). The religious perspective leaves us with a dilemma. How can we repent of things that happened to us as children, events not of our choosing, and often out of our control? Perhaps it's easier instead to understand forgiveness as a way of being rescued from our shame and guilt?

Over the last fifteen years there has been a growing psychological literature on the concept of forgiveness, and from a variety of perspectives. It tends to be thought about as something you consciously do – an action or an attitude that you can adopt as forgiver. The stated advantage is that overcoming negative feelings towards the other person will bring benefits to the forgiver. In this way the psychological literature seems to concentrate on forgiveness almost as an intellectual exercise in which the wronged person makes a decision to forgive; so it can become a powerful therapeutic or self-help intervention. There is occasional acknowledgement that the experience of forgiving involves more than just the interpersonal dimension, in that the action then opens up aspects of the forgiver to him- or herself, and inevitably a different view of the world.

Although forgiveness is a concept that is explored in some branches of therapy and counselling, it is not an idea that is theoretically entertained in psychoanalytic and psychodynamic work. In the index to the 24 volumes of Freud's works there is no entry for 'forgiveness'. The emphasis instead is on some form of integration of both good and bad aspects of the self and others. Inside ourselves we experience conflict. As Faust says, 'Two souls, alas, are housed within my breast.' Jung writes, 'Modern man has heard enough about guilt and sin. He is sorely enough beset by his own bad conscience, and wants rather to know how he is to reconcile himself with his own nature – how he is to love the enemy in his own heart.' [3]

The awareness of the coexistence of two opposing feelings of love and hate is a form of reconciliation of inner conflict. What does this mean? Imagine again the child in the last chapter waiting for his father's visit, and the father does not come. Move on thirty years to the now grown-up boy, whom we'll call Jim, as he arrives fifteen minutes late to pick up his own child from primary school. Jim's child is crying, cross, pleased and upset all at the same time. 'I thought you were never going to come', he says, and describes, as he both tries to hit and cuddle up to him, how he waited in the classroom for his father. This incident brings up for Jim the previously forgotten memory, and there are all the feelings laid out in the next generation.

Two scenarios are now possible. In one Jim shuts off the painful memory, tells his child to 'shut up' and 'hurry up' and stays in a bad mood with his son all evening. The child learns to repress and cut himself off from his feelings, and trusts his father a little less and fears him a little more. In the other possible scenario the child says what he feels, and Jim apologises and explains the delay. Although Jim could not express anything himself as a child about the betrayal, he can now remember how he still loved his father, even when he let him down. He can accept the upset and rage in his son because Jim is aware enough to realise that he felt both love and hate towards his father as a child. He understands that he felt a deep anger at his father's treatment of him. Years later he knows that his father was weak, and that, not wanting to upset his new wife, he sacrificed his relationship with Jim. Jim's forgiveness includes the recognition of having loved and hated his father, and both Jim and his son are released from the past.

This awareness of both love and hate in a relationship is a difficult place to reach and the analytic term used is ambivalence – mixed feelings. Yet the recognition of both loving and hateful feelings towards the same person leads to the possibility of recognition of their humanity and similarity to us. In this acceptance lies the potential for compassion and forgiveness. Perhaps it is at times as easy to mouth the words of forgiveness, as it is to superficially say sorry. That is not authentic or mature forgiveness. Really to move to a place of forgiveness and acceptance is a struggle, and one that needs to acknowledge our own self-absorption, and the power of our egoism.

Ambivalence allows us to keep both the good and bad aspects of the person who hurt us in mind, so we take in the experience of what happened, and all our feelings of fear, hate and shame, while accepting that the wrong was done by the adult. Sometimes the strength of our hateful feelings reflects the strength of the loving feelings that we once knew. We seek to understand why we were treated badly and the meaning of the way the adult behaved. If we can in turn pity the adult we can start to forgive – though not forget.

It seems that forgiveness has both a divine and a human outcome. It is a chance to reconnect parts of ourselves, and be reconciled to those from whom we are estranged. Asking for forgiveness is a route to reconnection with God.

Turn and be forgiven – finding acceptance

So that's the theory, but how do we turn and change our position so we open up and reconnect? In the last chapter the idea of conscious preoccupation was discussed in the context of a growing awareness of feelings. Conscious letting go starts to happen at the point when we are able to begin to accept our preoccupation with feelings of fear, anger, shame and guilt. This is part of the journeying home.

Revd David Bryant[4] writes that it's hard to scrape up any plus points for guilt with its link to self-loathing and inner conflict. For the religious it can be 'a form of self-aggrandisement – a spiritual ego trip'. He gives the example: 'Far from being insignificant, my sins are so important that they warrant the attention of God, even his wrath.' The church, he suggests, has in the past 'retained power by inducing guilt'. One way out – perhaps a way of turning – is through remorse. 'Unlike guilt, remorse is upbeat and positive. It starts with contrition, burgeons into expiation and is finalised in resolve. In other words, feel sorry, put matters right as far as possible, and move on.' His point is interesting as he places the emphasis on the shift from the suffocation of inner self-hatred to a reconnection with the outside world. Remorse springs from a genuine sense and appreciation of sorrow for what has happened and for the wrong done. Remorse would be a more helpful place than guilt, where one can be stuck, to begin to change perspective for those of us preoccupied with the past.

Closely connected to the appreciation of what has happened is the idea of acceptance both of who we are and what has happened to us. Perhaps if we begin to tell our story we can begin to feel accepted and acceptable within ourselves. It seems like a form of confession. The therapist contains, reframes and offers reasons why we feel as we do. Religious confession is different and we are offered divine forgiveness. 'Christ accepts us as we are,' wrote Walter Trobisch, 'but when he accepts us, we cannot remain as we are.'[5]

When the adult Thomas Merton became a Catholic he made his first confession, but some years later he felt ongoing shame about the life he had led prior to his conversion. He links this 'anguish of self-knowledge' to self-love and pride: 'It is pride that feels the burning of that shame.' He writes, 'I suddenly remembered who I was, who I had been. I was astonished: since last September I seemed to have forgotten that I had ever sinned.'[6] His journals and later writing document the inevitably gradual process of self-acceptance once he was accepted some years later as a Trappist monk.

We need gestures of acceptance from those who matter to us before we can begin the long path to accept ourselves and feel compassion for how we are. If as children we have not felt accepted for who we are, we look for disapproval, criticism and rejection in those we meet, especially from those in authority.

Kirsty's story

In talking about her childhood Kirsty had found her voice. Our meetings became a route away from the secrecy of the past into the public realm. In that sense Kirsty began to re-connect with the world. She needed to talk about what had happened to her as she grew up, and how she felt about her family life. Talking about feelings within the context of an accepting relationship served many functions. Kirsty didn't feel so lonely and isolated with her pain, so she stopped drinking so much. She felt less tense and a bit less self-punishing – she hated herself for herself a little less. As she talked about the past she felt she could understand a lot more, and could start to feel some genuine sense of sorrow for what had happened in her family.

I am going to focus on two incidents that happened several years into our work together. By this time, because of telling her story and being listened to, Kirsty was a great deal more confident and had begun to make new friends. However, there were often experiences when she met people and some-thing went wrong, and then the old patterns predominated. Kirsty would feel upset and turn on herself. She had begun to attend relaxation classes held in a local church hall. The classes were helping her regain a sense of ownership and feel better about her body. A woman ran these classes whom Kirsty liked very much and trusted.

When this leader was away for a week the class was taken over by someone else. Kirsty had immediately felt thrown by the change in the group – she instantly disliked the replacement. This I think was a displacement of her angry and upset feelings towards the original leader for letting her down by not being there. At the end of the class the group usually had refreshments and stayed for a chat with each other. As Kirsty reached for a second biscuit the replacement leader had joked that she was being greedy. Kirsty had felt deep anger at this remark and without thinking had turned and kicked the nearby cupboard door so hard it had splintered. Mortified by what she had done, she left, and now felt unable to return to the group.

When we thought about what had happened, Kirsty was able to link her feelings about being greedy with the feelings of neediness she had felt as a child. She had felt hungry for acceptance and love, and the incident with the second biscuit reactivated those feelings. She thought the replacement woman was too bossy in the class and in that sense she reminded Kirsty of her powerful father. The good leader (mother) had left her to the mercies of the bad leader (father/bully), who had then attacked Kirsty. However, the depths of her remorse lay in her own uncontrollable feelings of anger. This she had only known before within herself, and had turned on herself, but now her anger was displayed to everyone. As we slowly pieced it all together, Kirsty told me she felt a terrible recognition that perhaps in that way she was not so different from her violent father. In the aggressive action she discovered that she too had a temper. This recognition was the beginning of Kirsty's gradual easing of tension towards him. It was the seed of acceptance of who he was, and within that what he had done. It was not a condoning of his aggression in the family, but it was awareness and knowledge.

A further outcome of the incident at the relaxation class – the irony of it being a 'relaxing' experience we were able to laugh about later – emerged when Kirsty took responsibility for the splintered cupboard door. Feeling very worried, ill at ease and full of shame and remorse she went to speak to the Vicar, and was surprised at the accepting way in which he dealt with the matter. He said it was time the cupboard was replaced anyway! In the course of their discussion the Vicar suggested she might be interested in other activities going on in the same hall, and drew her attention to an open event on prayer. Amazed by his attitude towards her (inevitably Kirsty was expecting at least angry disapproval and rejection and a huge bill to pay), she found herself so embarrassed, relieved and grateful that she agreed to go, although adding that she didn't believe in God, and wouldn't be any good at praying.

Kirsty was extremely nervous about the event, but felt she should go because the Vicar had been kind to her about the cupboard. Acceptance from a man that was nothing to do with sex was a new experience for her, and part of her was intrigued. At our meeting after the event I was curious to hear what had happened. Kirsty had been in a small group, and as they introduced themselves, the Vicar had repeated each of their first names by saying, 'and God created *Kirsty* in his own image and saw that she was good'. This acceptance had reduced her to tears, and it had been a very emotional time for her. The possibility that she might be acceptable to other people and acceptable to God was overwhelming. As Kirsty said, 'to accept being lovable would be a huge thing.' The process of acceptance of who she was opened up the possibility of being acceptable to others, which in turn led to a deeper acceptance of herself, and of the difference and similarity between her and her father. Within this acceptance lay the potential seed for forgiveness and compassion.

As we forgive those who have wronged us

To be able to forgive those who have wronged and upset us we need not just the experience of acceptance, but also a genuine sense of the other person. In other words we need to be able to feel concern for someone different and separate from ourselves. This capacity develops alongside the recognition of the mixed feelings of love and hatred towards the same person, with both good and bad aspects. It helps us move on from suddenly feeling overwhelmed by another person's bad parts, so that we only experience the other person as completely hateful, and the loving feelings get lost. Inevitably, under pressure, we can sometimes re-experience that rather paranoid and cut off or restricted state of mind. It's easy to think of times, perhaps when stressed at work or on a course, when someone who seemed fine and friendly suddenly adopts a rather critical or dismissive tone, which overwhelms our previous good experience with them. Suddenly he or she has become totally hateful and someone to be avoided. Developing a capacity for concern means that the other person is loved despite the 'bad parts', and so love is sustained and can give us a sense of stability. In other words if we can begin to forgive those who have hurt us then we can start to separate out their harmful behaviour from their actual person.

Clearly some of us who have been hurt as children may still need to keep that person at a distance and not have too much, or even anything, to do with them. However, if we can be rescued from our sense of shame and guilt through a better understanding of the person and their behaviour and our own response to what happened, we are then able to separate from the internal preoccupation and live our own life apart from the person who caused us pain. We can begin to be more compassionate to ourselves.

Alan's story

In the last chapter we heard about Alan's bargain with God, and the depth of his anxiety and fear about his mother's and his own health. In a sense it seemed as if Alan had an overly developed capacity for concern in that he wasn't just anxious about his own health, but worried about the well-being of all those around him. This dynamic came to the fore in our meetings when I had to cancel my arrangement with him because of flu. When we next met, after a two-week break, Alan looked very pale and worried. He was suffering from strong head pains, and was frightened about what they might be. He told me that the agreement with God had broken down. He had done so much extra work and gone out of his way to be helpful, but his panic had got worse, and this time he felt sure his fears were real. Part of him thought that it was all the same old psychological stuff that we had been talking about, but another more powerful part of him was convinced that he had cancer. In a sense he felt it served him right for all the previous panics – now he *really* did have something wrong. In other words Alan was *really* punishing himself for something terrible that had taken place.

It took some time for Alan to become calm enough to try and think through what was happening in his mind. In a sense something terrible had taken place. I had abandoned Alan in a way that reminded him of the times in his childhood that he had felt abandoned after his mother became ill. Although the adult-part of him registered that I had flu, it was a short step for that to become something more serious in the child-part of his mind. Flu might mean that I would die, and then he would be totally abandoned. In other words Alan was back in touch with the terrified, vulnerable baby-part of himself that had experienced that first trauma at eighteen months when his mother left him. At that age he had felt overwhelmed by his experiences, thinking she had gone for ever. He had had insufficient language skills to understand what was happening, and so his experiences were expressed physically – the only way available. His present head pains were largely stress-induced, but also represented the painful and conflictual thinking about being left and coping alone.

Alan was left at the age when small children are beginning to understand that they are separate from the mothering person. It is a time for exploring what's 'me' and what's 'not-me'. Alan's trauma occurred at this sensitive time, so part of him was left not knowing what was his and what belonged to someone else. In other words the boundary between himself and, in this first instance, his mother was unclear. Separation between mother and baby was forced by circumstance, and part of Alan had never recovered from the experience. He was left feeling that illness in another person was his responsibility, and so he was placed in a powerful omnipotent position in his close relationships.

In that sense Alan's apparent caring persona was a way of managing. His capacity for concern was not genuinely based on appreciation and acceptance of the other person as separate from himself. Alan was still in charge; his inner world was constellated around a desperate attempt not to repeat the earlier trauma when he had felt such loss. The apparent solution to keep everyone well (through Alan's acts of penance) was now the problem, and God had failed to live up to his side of the bargain. Alan's God was also very much under Alan's control, imaged as a useful partner in keeping Alan's precarious sense of self alive.

Some years later when Alan had worked through a great deal of his childhood experiences, he asked God for help with accepting how his mother had been. He wanted to feel able to visit and talk to her without resentment. He wanted to let go of the complicated structures that he had built up to protect himself, so he could live differently. He wanted to feel forgiven for his own angry feelings, and to be able to forgive both his parents. This *wanting* is part of the process of *turning* to be forgiven. Alan spoke of a gradually changing perception of his mother. Instead of this powerful figure who needed to be kept well and placated by good behaviour, Alan could see a rather vulnerable, physically frail, ageing woman. This shift in how he saw and experienced his mother helped him feel some sympathy and understanding towards her, and so he could start to forgive her for leaving him all those years ago.

The prodigal child

The story of the prodigal son is a story about acceptance and forgiveness. It is about acceptance and forgiveness of a kind and on a scale that we can barely access. It is also about being given something – the son is given acceptance and forgiveness by the father. Here is the chance to 'love God for what he gives us', the second stage of St Bernard's journey home. The father in the story is free from recriminations and accusations. He runs to his child as soon as he sees that his son has turned towards home, and clasps him in his arms. The forgiveness described is genuine and total. The father has no shadow or hidden part that desires to punish or undermine. To the contrary he gives his prodigal child gifts and celebrates his return with a party. The younger son is completely forgiven for his aggressive rejection of the father, and the elder son is forgiven for his resentment and jealousy. The story tells us that divine love and forgiveness is everlasting and unconditional – it is something we can graciously experience, but can barely begin to emulate. In Karl Barth's view, Jesus' gift of forgiveness, of grace, was more astonishing than Jesus' miracles. For while miracles broke the physical laws of the universe, forgiveness broke the moral rules.[7]

We can speculate on how both the sons in the story felt when they were left alone together once the celebration for the return of the younger son was over. For example, would it have been possible for the elder son to overcome his resentment that the younger brother had avoided all the work?

Could the younger son sufficiently confront his own guilt and self-recrimination, and accept his father's love and forgiveness? These are the familiar human emotions that are so difficult to deal with. Without the presence of the father, could the brothers forgive each other and themselves? Sometimes there can be a vicious circle – it's not possible to forgive until we feel forgiven. Who is going to break first? There can be great fear about rejection or further hurt. In the story the father transcends such fear and gives the brothers and us an example to follow.

Henri Nouwen writes about the generosity needed to move from fear to love. Grief, forgiveness and generosity are, he writes, 'three ways to a truly compassionate fatherhood'. To forgive we often need to

> climb over the wall of arguments and angry feelings . . . it is a wall of fear of being used or hurt again. It is a wall of pride, and the desire to stay in control . . . Forgiveness is the way to step over the wall and welcome others into my heart without expecting anything in return. Only when I remember that I am the Beloved Child can I welcome those who want to return with the same compassion as that with which the Father welcomes me.[8]

Often as adults we are left with unfinished business and a desire to mend relationships that fragmented years earlier. Marie Tighe describes her feelings on hearing about a life-threatening condition and impending surgery. 'My greatest concern was to forgive and be forgiven. Nothing seemed to matter more than being reconciled with an estranged friend with whom I had had a bitter disagreement. Once this reconciliation was accomplished, I was filled with peace and joy which blotted out any sadness.'[9] Strangely, despite the earlier ultrasound evidence and the gloomy prognosis, the subsequent surgery revealed there was nothing wrong, and Marie Tighe goes on to describe events over the following decade that eventually allowed her to discover in a deeper way that God's love is unconditional.

In among our preoccupation with the past, and the preoccupation with our fear, guilt and shame, lies, I believe, a longing for something to be different. The seeds for change and movement are, as acknowledged at the end of the last chapter, included in the besieged state. By starting to turn our mind towards something other, healing becomes possible – 'turn and be forgiven'. Forgiveness arises out of healing as a process of discovery. The discovery takes the form of a gradual easing of tension both within oneself and towards the person who, we feel, has wronged us. It is not something to be achieved or something that we can learn to reduce our pain. It is something that begins to happen to us when we allow ourselves to become more open to transformation. 'The first and often the only person to be healed by forgiveness is the person who does the forgiveness . . . When we genuinely forgive, we set a prisoner free and then discover that the prisoner we set free was us.'[10]

If we can unlock the door and move out of the prison of hating ourselves for ourselves enough to be given something different, then it is possible to shift some of the hate to love. In that sense St Bernard's degrees of love are not static achieved positions but rather deepening spirals of awareness and recognition. Each time we allow ourselves to receive something good we can lessen our self-hatred. This is part of the journeying home.

CHAPTER FOUR

State of oppression

IN THE NEXT two chapters we look at another story to help our spiritual recovery from a troubled past. This is based on the biblical accounts of life under Pharaoh in Egypt, and then the exodus from Egypt, and is a story of oppression and liberation. The route of guilt and forgiveness explored in the previous two chapters, with the example of Peter's story and the story of the paralysed man, tended to focus on expression of the troubled past through body symptoms and the body image. On this route the focus is rather more on how we think and understand what has happened to us, in other words what goes on in our mind. This chapter looks at what happens to our thinking when we are shocked and afraid, and how this can affect our relationship with God. In Chapter 5 ways of relieving this deficit and damage are discussed, in order that we can regain the ability to think for ourselves. If we cannot think straight, then how can we entertain the thought of a loving and compassionate God? If we cannot bear to think at all, then how can there be anything other than getting through life as best we can? We need to know what we think as well as what we feel on our journeying home.

The story of oppression and liberation

The Exodus story is a story of slavery and bondage, then liberation, a journey and a destination. This was the prime narrative for the people of ancient Israel. In Deuteronomy we find the core of the longer story found in the first five books of the Hebrew Scriptures. 'Then you shall say to your children, "We were Pharaoh's slaves in Egypt, but the Lord brought us out of Egypt with a mighty hand. The Lord displayed before our eyes great and awesome signs and wonders against Egypt, against Pharaoh and all his household. He brought us out from there in order to bring us in, to give us the land that he promised on oath to our ancestors' (Deuteronomy 6:21–23).

As Borg[1] reminds us, the story was repeated and celebrated, especially at the annual festival of Passover. It was seen not simply as a story about the past, but as a story about the present. The Passover liturgy confirms that this is a story that can apply to 'us, too, the living': 'It was not only our ancestors that the Holy One, blessed be God, redeemed; us, too, the living, God redeemed together with them.'[2]

The first part of the story of Exodus describes life for the Hebrew slaves under the control of Pharaoh. It is characterised by forced labour, an attitude of ruthlessness on the part of those in charge, and infanticide. There are meagre rations and much misery: 'The Israelites groaned under their slavery, and cried out' (Exodus 2:23). God hears the misery of the slaves and appoints Moses as the leader of the Israelites. The narrative then moves through the plagues and the departure from Egypt. Liberation, though, is a long-drawn-out process. As the people emerge from the control of Pharaoh they move into the wilderness and a journey that lasts for forty years. The destination of the journey is the Promised Land – the place of God's presence.

The Exodus story can be recognised also in the New Testament. The meaning of Jesus' life, death and resurrection can be seen in terms of Jesus overcoming powers that captivate and restrict us, such as wrongdoing, illness and death. When Jesus expresses love and compassion 'he is as it were an embodiment of the homeward journey'.[3] We know that the idea of 'the journey' as a metaphor for understanding an individual's spiritual life is widespread and covers many religious traditions. Here we are also using it as a metaphor for releasing ourselves from the pain of the past, learning to love and accept ourselves and, if we can, allowing spiritual awakening.

The diagnosis of what is wrong, according to this second story, lies in the unconscious and conscious preoccupation with a past that leaves us imprisoned in a particular way of thinking or, as it sometimes turns out, not-thinking. In other words for some people imprisoned in the past, it is like living in Egypt, a place of bondage. It is as if there is 'a Pharaoh' lodged in our mind that controls our very thoughts and way of thinking. This is a figure that oppresses us, and yet from whom we are reluctant to break free. The necessary prescription, discussed in the next chapter, is liberation leading to a capacity to think for oneself.

'Always on my mind'

In the book and the film *About a Boy* we grow to understand the experience of Marcus, a twelve-year-old who finds his mother after she has made a suicide attempt. 'But this was the scariest thing he'd ever seen, by a million miles, and he knew the moment he walked in that it was something he'd have to think about forever.' Months later, Will (played by Hugh Grant in the film), who has befriended Marcus, asks whether his mum is OK, and then 'Does it bother you?'

> He'd never talked about it since the night it happened, and even then he'd never said what he felt. What he felt, all the time, every single day, was a horrible fear. In fact, the main reason he came round to Will's after school was that he was able to put off going back to the flat; he could no longer climb the stairs at home without looking at his feet and remembering the Dead Duck Day. By the time

he got to the bit where he had to put his key in the lock, his heart was thumping in his chest and his arms and his legs, and when he saw his mum watching the news or cooking or preparing work on the dining table, it was all he could do not to cry, or be sick, or something.

'A bit, when I think about it.'

'How often do you think about it?'

'I dunno.'

All the time, all the time, all the time.[4]

In Marcus's experience, as with other damaged children, there can be no psychic trauma without a feeling of powerlessness real or remembered, and there can be no feeling of powerlessness without a feeling of danger. His anxiety as he returns home is almost an 'alarm signal' set off by his mind in order to prevent the situation from becoming traumatic again, and to allow useful defence measures to be taken in time. Later in this chapter, in Alan's story, we can see how such defensive anxiety, initially an apparent solution, can sometimes become so dominant that it turns into a problem in its own right.

Lenore Terr is an American psychiatrist who has spent her working life documenting the psychological effects of verifiable childhood trauma. She writes, 'Psychic trauma appears to leave an indelible mark in a child's mind, no matter how young he is when the trauma strikes.'[5] It is very apparent that a child's perception and thinking are affected by overwhelming external events, though clearly thinking cannot be isolated from feeling and from behaviour. Dr Terr notes how serious childhood difficulties and trauma are often first recorded as visualisations, or even, by the youngest infants, as feeling sensations, before they can be recorded as words – or thoughts. In other words we retain visual images of what has happened to us, or we record the impact physically even if we cannot remember.

If our experiences in childhood are very damaging and cumulative then as children and later as adults we may

become psychically numb, or completely cut off and dissociated both from what has happened and from any
subsequent thinking about what has happened. It is as if the
experiences are so overwhelming that our very capacity to
even start to manage them packs up and so we become frozen
through the events. In adulthood this can lead to an almost
permanent state of detachment, sometimes affecting both
body and mind. This is a state of mind beyond expression,
beyond feeling and beyond thought – a place of total
imprisonment, a place of solitary confinement.

> I am shut in so that I cannot escape;
> My eye grows dim through sorrow.
>
> (Psalm 88:8b–9a)

This mindset is then brought to any and all relationships
including any potential relationship with God. As Shengold
(1985) writes, '*too* much neglect and *too* much torment and
abuse (especially when these are *too* early) make for the blank
slate of devastated psychic structure . . . It is all too easy to
murder the souls as well as the bodies of children.'[6]

In terms of the stages of relief and recovery described earlier
in the book, the state of oppression described in this story
can be an unconscious preoccupation – in other words we
do not appreciate that our thinking is so restricted by past
relationships. It may be that we adopt a state of not thinking
at all, and do not realise this. It also can be something that
we start to perceive through our present relationship difficulties and contemporary events – in other words it becomes a
conscious preoccupation and we begin to see how we are
affected. We can see that as a result of a troubled childhood
we are diminished in the way we can think, and think of
living, and mostly we long to change and escape from this
oppressive captivity. If we think about this in terms of St
Bernard's degrees of love, this state of mind may be about
not knowing whether we love or hate ourselves – we just
exist, but in limbo.

The master–slave relationship

In the Exodus story Pharaoh is cunning and also at times seductive, although he is involved in manipulation, emotional blackmail and dehumanising practices. Although Pharaoh is powerful, sometimes he can be tricked. Within the big story of oppression and liberation there are other smaller stories, such as the story of the clever midwives in Exodus 1:8–22. Shiphrah and Puah are ordered to implement Pharaoh's policy of genocide by killing the Israelites' babies when they are born. First of all they ignore his orders but, when summoned to explain what's going on, they employ quick thinking and make a joke which Pharaoh believes. They come away unscathed and Pharaoh gives up on the midwives and gets the general populace to do his dirty work for him instead. The two women show that sometimes it is still possible to think differently and make a choice even within a state of oppression. We too can sometimes trick our 'inner Pharaoh' or see it as a caricature, or almost as a joke, and gain a glimpse of how we might be different.

Any state of oppression involves a master and a slave, and a relationship between the two. In this section I want to explore this dynamic, or this inner relationship as we experience it in our mind, and our oppressed restricted thinking.

Obviously our thinking as children is hugely affected by our parents or parenting figures: we take in everything that goes on around us, in our immediate environment, and that includes the way we experience the grown-ups who look after and care for us. This clearly diffuses as we get older and friends, teachers, clergy and the outside world influence us. However, the lives of those who have grown up in the charge of cruel, crazy, inconsistent and self-absorbed parents, or parent substitutes, are subject to living a form of mastery and submission that lasts well into adulthood. In other words, the way we have experienced those significant people around us is taken in and becomes part of the way we think, it becomes part of our internal world. The internal world and our mindset as children can also be dramatically affected by a single disastrous event, when the event or other person involved becomes all-absorbing and affects our subsequent thinking, behaviour and development. For some of us it is as if part of our very being is stuck in the past and in a regressed place and time that can be traced back to particular stressful events.

What is going on in the mind of the master? Pharaoh, as the story explains, needed the slaves. The concept of mastery inevitably involves a relationship with another – initially externally (Pharaoh used the slaves to provide cheap labour), then as an internalised configuration or way of thinking (the slaves as they became more numerous were perceived as a possible threat and needed more controlling). Mastery reflects a wish to ignore or neutralise the other person's needs, and just see the person as somebody to be used. There is no space for the slave/victim to be seen as different, or have wishes or thoughts of their own separate from the master/adult. This links back to the idea described in the last chapter about the capacity for concern. The Pharaoh figure has no capacity for concern for the person that they are oppressing. The victim is only seen as someone who can satisfy the needs of the Pharaoh. This is a very powerful experience for both parties, and is often not recognised by either – in other words it just becomes a way of life. If it is something that we live every day as children, it just becomes 'the way that it is'. As we read in the story of Exodus, until God intervened through speaking and instructing Moses there seemed no alternative to the state of oppression. In other words, we often need something or someone outside ourselves, and beyond ourselves, to help us to achieve release from a besieged state.

The powerful dynamics resulting from a troubled childhood become part of us. They become just the way we are, and part of the way we think. More worryingly they become what we expect from relationships. It's then easy to see that our longing for affection and acceptance becomes associated with the ill-treatment, or intrusive parenting, or the abandoning parent, or whatever was seen as 'normal' in the family. Love becomes associated with pain, or if separation from the parent has been part of the childhood trauma, then love and separation become inextricably connected. It is sadly familiar that if our parents have hurt us we tend to seek out others who will hurt us in the same way. Why does this happen? It seems that by repeating what has happened to us in the past we can paradoxically feel safe and can imagine our parents' presence. In other words, if we keep everything the same and familiar, we do not have to change and face up to all the messy feelings that we have.

Sophie, the teenager who wrote poetry, expected history to repeat itself in all her relationships. At one point she was so frightened of meeting anyone in case they hurt her that she could not leave her home. Sometimes she would venture out quickly to a shop but she felt safest in bed with the door locked, watching television. She needed at all costs to protect herself. Part of her difficulty was that her parents had been responsible for the traumas that occurred and as a small child she had believed in them.

After all, if the trauma or the difficulties involved a parent or close relative, then who can be blamed? If, as children, we found ourselves in a position where we could have complained, or resisted what was happening, then more likely than not we risked rejection and further obliteration. As young children, if we are neglected or traumatised, or in an emotionally debilitating relationship with a parent, we naturally think that this is how families are, and that this happens to all children. This thought only changes once we are older and have a different experience, and visit and see other families, or talk about it. The physical or emotional domination by the adult places us as children in a position of passivity and weakness with a disregard of pain, denial and unhappiness, and this experience becomes part of our mindset.

It is easy to remember how big adults felt to us when we were small children, and how powerful older children seemed. Imagine then the impossibility of taking these figures on and resisting whatever ill-treatment is taking place. It is not just that as children we are smaller and younger: there is also something very powerful about another person's needs completely dominating us. In such a relationship we can become passive, and anyway it seems as if we have very little choice in what is happening. One of the most disturbing aspects of events such as sexual abuse, especially within the home, is that in the process of denying the needs and wishes of the child there is an aspect of unification: 'This special relationship is what we both want, this is how it is.' Such a state of oppression clearly precludes choice and, as I want to stress, precludes the freedom to think.

So what is the effect of all this on any potential relationship with God? If we stop thinking or only think in a very restricted way about our other relationships, how can we see ourselves as worthy to be given to by God? In the context of spiritual life and belief, it is of course possible to transfer the dynamic interplay of Pharaoh and the slave to our relationship with God. Without thinking about it and without any conscious recognition we simply continue our present preoccupation and mindset, but substitute God for the oppressive figure that hurt us. In that way nothing has changed, we have merely reinforced our expectations of how relationships work, and imaged God in a deeply familiar way. In other words we see God as a figure that does not care for us and has no interest in our needs.

> 'He has sent me to proclaim release to the captives
> and recovery of sight to the blind,
> to let the oppressed go free . . .'

God's message (Isaiah 61:1–2), spoken again by Christ (Luke

4:18), to set the prisoner free, passes by unheard and unseen in favour of an older and safer pattern.

In Chapter 1, I quoted George Orwell's school experiences of corporal punishment. Leonard Shengold refers to Orwell's book *1984* as 'a veritable primer on soul murder'.[7] The book is, then, not just a commentary on a totalitarian society, but rather demonstrates some of the after-effects of being subject to chronic neglect and repeated abuse as a child at the hands of tyrannical adults, in this case Orwell's schoolteachers and his school matron. In the book *1984*, Big Brother and the Thought Police aim to control the freedom to think, and abolish the concept of freedom: 'there will *be* no thought . . . Orthodoxy means not thinking – not needing to think. Orthodoxy is unconsciousness.' Despite this expectation, George Orwell has his central character Winston Smith note a sense of something different: 'Always in your stomach and in your skin there was a sort of protest, a feeling that you had been cheated of something that you had a right to.'

The powerful person (adult) holds sway, and Winston Smith's response to torture (abuse) is to give in to his tormentor O'Brien, and finally agree with his thinking that he sees five fingers rather than the actual four. 'For a moment he clung to O'Brien like a baby, curiously comforted by the heavy arm round his shoulders. He had the feeling that O'Brien was his protector, that the pain was something that came from outside, from some other source, and that it was O'Brien that would save him from it.'

In the book the tormentor describes this rethinking or brainwashing in the following way: 'Never again will you be capable of ordinary human feeling. Everything will be dead inside you. Never again will you be capable of love, or friendship, or joy of living, or laughter, or curiosity, or courage, or integrity. You will be hollow. We shall squeeze you empty, and then we shall fill you with ourselves.'[8]

This denial of oneself can be seen sometimes in people, like Kirsty, who wondered whether the bullying and marital violence she had witnessed had happened to another little girl. This is a form of denial of awareness, or partial dissociation – a way of coping. Imagine how much mental pain there must be to lead to a state of thinking where part of us needs to believe that what we suffered happened to another. Another term to describe this experience is 'doublethink'. This is a term coined by George Orwell to describe a state of oppression that involves both knowing and yet not knowing at the same time, and believing something and then forgetting it and believing something else. He writes of being 'conscious of complete truthfulness while telling carefully-constructed lies, [holding] simultaneously two opinions which cancelled out, knowing them to be contradictory and believing in both of them'.[9]

Kirsty's story and the place of 'not thinking'

In the last chapter we heard about the difficulties Kirsty sometimes experienced when things went wrong in friendships. At the beginning of our work together she found it hard to think about what happened – she tended to just react to situations. Her life seemed a series of disconnected events and she had little feeling for herself as a child. That is why the incident with the cupboard door, described in the last chapter, was so helpful, because Kirsty was by then able to begin to make links and connections between the past and the present. She also began to be responsible for what she was feeling and doing. In this sense her state of oppression characterised by not thinking moved to a place of freedom to think.

What does it mean to 'not think'? When Kirsty described events in her family it was tempting to reduce explanations of how unhappy she was just to the external events. 'I am like this because my father drank and was violent.' However, her experiences were also registered in her mind, and in the way she did not think about herself and other people. It was very hard for Kirsty to properly register what she wanted and what she felt; and even what she had done and what had been done to her. When we first began meeting, Kirsty would often say 'I don't know' in response to any enquiry about how she felt. She would sometimes add, 'You tell me – I haven't a clue.' She was used to someone else telling her what to do and how to be. It seemed that to get in touch and make meaning of what she felt brought with it a threat of falling apart – a threat of disintegration.

One of the reasons that Kirsty found it hard to think was because she had felt very frightened as a child. Her father, a big man, had also been dangerous, especially when he was drunk and aggressive. Kirsty had seen the bruises on her mother, and indeed had also been hit sometimes by her father, as had the other children. Kirsty had also been neglected, not just because her mother had felt too low and defeated to manage and care for the children, but also because neither parent had been able to offer her an example of how to mentally represent what she was feeling. Neither parent, from Kirsty's recollections, had really ever spoken about what went on between them or with the children. Kirsty had turned her feelings onto her own body, as she had no other way of expressing what she felt.

If you cannot think about your own feelings then you are also impaired in your ability to think about what might be going on for anyone else. This makes relationships very unsafe. You cannot really begin to imagine what might be happening in the mind of another person, or what they might be feeling. The capacity for concern for another is not possible. If we are really to manage our feelings then we need to start to put our sense of them into words. We need to be able to think, and describe, even if just to ourselves, what we feel. This is especially important so that, when terrible things happen to us, we are not overwhelmed by them and do not fall apart. It is also crucial when we start to form close relationships. The development of this capacity to represent

76

what is happening inside us is dependent on a degree of consistency and safety in early infancy and childhood and good-enough psychic functioning in the parents.[10] By this I mean that our parents or the significant adults around us need to demonstrate their own ability to think about feelings so we can learn as children how to do it.

A further reason why Kirsty could not think lay in her preoccupation about whether any sexual interference or abuse had taken place with her father. I understood that it felt too worrying to think about the mind of her father, and how he might have perceived her. There is always doubt in how we remember the past. It is sometimes very difficult to know what actually happened. As Kirsty began to take responsibility for how she currently registered the past and present in her mind, she began to understand that she had used her developing sexuality in adolescence as a powerful weapon to undermine and take on her father. As memories emerged from the stuck state she recalled a sense that she had frightened him by her sexuality and the boys she attracted. He had, she remembered, once tried to touch her breasts, but after that had resorted to insults as she sought refuge in tough young men as protection from him.

This larger-than-life, aggressive, inconsistent father had filled Kirsty's mind and left her, initially unconsciously and then consciously, preoccupied with him. In the context of the Exodus story he was a tyrannical and all-powerful Pharaoh. He was someone from whom Kirsty longed to escape emotionally, but whom she was also anxious about letting go. In that sense she felt bound to him, and felt very lost at his death. In the next chapter we look at how Kirsty gradually liberated herself from this state of oppression, and allowed space for her own thoughts and ideas. She needed to acquire a language and a way of thinking about what she was feeling, and we began to do that by mapping out her past on paper. We look at this process in detail as part of how she gained the freedom to think.

The function of the plagues

In the Exodus story the plagues are sent as signs to show that something different is possible and has to happen to break the stalemate. The signs are revealed to both Pharaoh and the Hebrews, and eventually lead to the breaking up of the state of oppression. The endless succession of plagues: water turned to blood, frogs, flies, boils, hailstones, locusts, darkness, and death of the firstborn wear down the opposition and power of the Pharaoh. Finally he begs the Hebrew slaves to leave. In the context of the stages of unconscious and conscious preoccupation, the plagues can be seen as small but powerful and relentless signs that the besieged internal state is beginning to break up. They are the irritating cracks that eventually appear in the strongest of defences, and ultimately wear down resistance to change.

Freud famously wrote about the return of the repressed, a process whereby what has been pushed down out of our consciousness remains indestructible and therefore tends to reappear, often by rather distorted or devious routes. Sometimes this is through similar occurrences – such as that described in the last chapter, when Jim was late to pick up his child from school and this reminded him of his own experience of waiting for his father. At other times changes in circumstances can weaken the defences and allow disallowed thoughts and painful memories to re-emerge. Perhaps, like Sarah, described in Chapter 1, a visit back to where we lived as children can lead to powerful feelings from the past.

The re-emergence of apparently long-forgotten feelings may be especially forceful when the repressed involves forbidden feelings of anger or sexuality. Freud comments on an etching by a then contemporary artist Felicien Rops.

> An ascetic monk has fled, no doubt from the temptations of the world, to the image of the crucified Saviour. And now the cross sinks down like a shadow, and in its place,

radiant, there arises instead the image of a voluptuous, naked woman, in the same crucified attitude. Other artists with less psychological insight have, in similar representations of temptation, shown Sin, insolent and triumphant, in some position alongside of the Saviour on the cross. Only Rops has placed Sin in the very place of the Saviour on the cross. He seems to know that, when what has been repressed returns, it emerges from the repressing force itself.[11]

In other words the very strong measures to keep certain feelings out of our thoughts may themselves crack, and placing God as a defence against what we are trying not to think about doesn't work. In the end what has been repressed needs to be brought to conscious awareness and recognised for what it is, otherwise we become preoccupied and restricted by our attempts to keep underlying upsetting, forbidden or frightening feelings at bay. It requires a great deal of psychic energy to keep repressed feelings out of mind. While Freud's aim was modest, 'to convert neurotic misery to common unhappiness',[12] Jung called his method a prospective one, a way to self-knowledge using all the potentialities of the psyche. He thought that the psyche was ultimately seeking for health and wholeness, especially in the second half of life. The urge to make changes can be provided by an illness, 'but just as often it comes from a desire to find a meaning in life, to restore one's lost faith in God and oneself'.[13] Such a desire is also a crack in the defences, a force or 'plague' that starts to break down the stuck state of oppression and restricted thinking, and leads to our longing to break free.

Alan's story – anxiety and magic thinking

In this part of Alan's story I want to return to his symptoms as described in the earlier chapter, and explore the thinking that led to their emergence. Alan, as we know, was very anxious and had adopted a form of magic thinking to assuage his feelings of anxious insecurity. 'If I do this then that won't happen (I or someone I need won't die).' His thinking was impaired because of his anxiety, and his state of oppression characterised as a state of subjective insecurity. Alan was not initially conscious of having fallen into this state of mind. As a small child he was able to react to these states of uneasiness without having acquired any concept of them. His thinking was replaced by conditioned reflexes, and had become established before he had acquired language. Originally the cause of his insecurity as an infant was the enforced absence of his mother, and his separation from her when she was ill, and he most needed her care and protection.

Whenever the adult Alan became anxious, even over something trivial or imagined, it related to the memory of his experienced childhood difficulties. This confirms the psychological understanding that the subjective value of our experiences far outweighs their perceived objective value. When I had flu, the adult Alan understood this as a minor event, but the child part of Alan felt the threat of enforced separation and this made the present feel terrible. His feeling of helplessness was overwhelming, in fact more so than the powerlessness experienced by a so-called normal person exposed to actual serious danger. For Alan the anticipated future was dangerous, and his past was dominated by painful events, and this led to an ever-anxious present. He was also stuck in this familiar state of oppression, as any change generated more anxious uncertainty.

Alan's anxiety originated in his early childhood and kept pulling him back into childhood. Alan had no clear memories of what had happened at eighteen months, and yet its troublesome consequences kept recurring. Part of our work to free his thinking was to re-establish this memory. He gradually understood that the present intensity of panic belonged to this earliest separation, a time when he had no words to use to help manage his dreadful, helpless feelings – feelings that had led to a form of psychic death. Alan's feelings of insecurity generated anxiety, and then when this became intolerable it led to further insecurity.

Any reassurance was futile and could be quickly undermined by the panicky child part of Alan whose thinking seemed captivated by this one special anxiety-producing idea of being abandoned and left helpless. Disaster was endlessly anticipated and this too was part of his magic thinking. It was his attempt to cope with and ward off the waves of helpless insecurity: if Alan knew the disaster that lay ahead he would not be caught off guard in the way he had experienced at eighteen months. This meant that Alan lurched from anticipated disaster to anticipated disaster, dragging his God along with him. He lived in a state of moral masochism, in which pain was always mixed with joy, suffering with pleasure. If things went well for a few days Alan became worried – 'it was all going too well.' If he felt happy Alan's anxiety also rose, as feeling happy both evoked the sense of impending disaster and potentially made the disaster more poignant and painful.

Often when anxiety is high then rationality and logic disappear. Alan's thinking was superstitious, and it was this superstition that he brought to his relationship with God. Alan's omnipotence of thought was based on his fear of his own annihilation. He projected his magic thinking onto God, who became a manifestation of Alan's egocentricity. Alan's fear of malevolent illness created a malevolent God who controlled him. He attributed a structure to reality that corresponded to his own regressed mental structure. As Charles Odier comments, 'The phobic patient appears as a kind of anxious god who constructs a malevolent reality to which he then adjusts himself as well as possible.'[14] Alan's anxiety was ultimately tied to the idea of death, and as Alan created God in his image he perpetuated this anxious attachment to death, denying any possibility of resurrection in the absence of anxiety.

Such neurotic regressed thinking only took up part of Alan's mind, and in the next chapter we see how he gradually released himself from the bondage of his extreme fear, and freed up his belief in himself and his belief in a different sort of God from the one he had decreed.

The prodigal child

In the story of the prodigal son the state of oppression is summed up in the younger son's experiences working as a hired hand feeding the pigs and starved of all nurture and support. However the impaired thinking is also found in his reckless spending and 'dissolute living'. Here we see someone behaving in a reactive fashion, determined to be the opposite of his loving father and his conformist elder brother (no mention of mother). How can the younger son define himself, except in opposition to what he has known in his family life? He cannot think for himself, only by angry actions that he imagines will hurt and upset his relatives. As his money runs out and his popularity fades, he is rejected. In his misguided attempt to find himself he discovers that he is nobody and experiences an intense loneliness. As he watches the herd of pigs he is in a place of defeated submission. He cannot think of a way out or what to do.

When we are in a state where we cannot think or think in a distorted way we are estranged from our true self. As prodigal children we are captivated by our own misery and deprivation, and cannot dare or bear to think that anything could be different. We keep our own inner Pharaoh in power and on the throne, rather than risk changing the familiar. Our insecurity is our security, and the panic, anxiety or symptoms we have devised almost seem to serve the function of helping us know that we are alive.

Sophie, the troubled teenager who wrote poetry, found it extremely difficult to speak about her state of mind, but found some relief in writing and then allowing me to read what she had written. She summed up her experiences in this way:

> A prisoner behind invisible bars
> Filled deep with emotional scars,
> Trapped forever by my mind,
> Peace within I cannot find.

She described her state of mind as a 'life sentence', where 'the prison gates were too high' and 'the key had been thrown away'. Writing the poems and sharing them with someone new was the beginning of unlocking this state of captivity.

Although cracks and openings appear in the false self that we build up to protect us from past pain and future uncertainty, we often need someone else to help show us the way to liberation. In the next chapter we look at how thinking can begin to change and develop and respond to new interventions and experiences.

CHAPTER FIVE

Freedom to think

Not understanding what has happened prevents us from going on to something better.[1]

WHAT DOES FREEDOM to think mean? In this context, it is about an openness and capability to be responsible for how the past and present are currently registered in the mind. This capacity to think through what has happened to us in the past, and how it affects us in the present, is a long and hard-won process. This is not about self-indulgent self-absorption or introspective navel-gazing. It is about fully developing the ability to mentally represent feeling states and sensations, and analysing and integrating them in a way that allows us to let go of the past, and live in the present free from fear of the future. The Passover liturgy quoted in the previous chapter included the phrase 'all of us must *think* of ourselves as having gone forth from Egypt' (my emphasis). The analysis and integration needed to think about what lies behind us involves a combination of emotion and intellect, feeling and thinking, body sensation and mind. It is owning who one is, and all that contributes to that identity.

So, how do we free our thinking? Using the idea of the four stages of relief outlined in Chapter 1, this part of the journey involves conscious letting go of restrictive or prescriptive thinking, leading in time to unconscious letting go. We need to free our thinking as part of the development of authentic faith and a mature relationship with God, so we can allow ourselves to receive and love God for what he gives us.

In this chapter we come back to the biblical narrative of the Exodus from Egypt, and pick up two central aspects of the story as it links to healing and recovery. The first is that of the leader, Moses, who led the people away from Egypt and the state of oppression. The second is the time in the wilderness and the potential pitfalls that existed there.

Getting help from a guide

In the Exodus story the liberation from slavery begins in the darkness following the death of the Egyptian firstborn. In a metaphorical sense when we are captivated by past pain and conflict we have to break free through 'killing off' our attachment to our imprisoned state of mind, and separating from the obstacles that prevent us from moving on. This may take place in desperation, or in a state of darkness or ignorance. Suddenly we have a feeling that something needs to change, and has to happen, and so a deeper part of our self responds to that feeling. In the same way that we may have an inner Pharaoh who oppresses us, it is also possible that we have an inner Moses who can help lead us to freedom. This may be a deep and genuine part of ourselves, uncorrupted by trauma and childhood difficulties, of which we slowly become aware. It may also, like Moses, initially be a very reluctant and resistant part of ourselves, and a part of us that feels ill-equipped and uncertain about what to do on this journey to freedom.

In his writing Thomas Merton, whose experiences have been thought about in earlier chapters, often refers to the idea of the 'true' self or 'real' self. This is different from the illusory and false self that, he feels, 'we have created by our habits of selfishness and by our constant flights from reality'.[2] He

85

writes that, 'We are created for freedom, for the options and self-dedications implied by the highest kind of love. We discover and develop our freedom precisely by making those decisions which take us out of ourselves to meet others as they really are.'[3] Thomas Merton explains that ultimately the Spirit of God teaches us the way of freedom by which we find out who we really are.

This idea of the true and false self is returned to in further detail in the next two chapters. However, if we can be open and receptive, the Spirit of God may speak directly to us; or may help awaken our recognition of our inner Moses. God reassured Moses that he would guide him. In the context of understanding our past, the Spirit of God may lead us to seek out an actual external someone who can help us, a contemporary Moses – a person such as vicar, spiritual director, counsellor or therapist that can help show us the way and activate our inner Moses.

An interesting aspect of the debate over whether therapists have taken the place of clergy is found in Freud's noted identification with the figure of Moses. This was a powerful theme in Freud's thinking about himself and his religious views, and he wrote a number of papers based on his study of Moses' life and character. In 1901 he had first seen Michelangelo's statue of Moses in Rome, and returned to look at it over the years before publishing an anonymous study of the statue in 1914. In 1909 Freud's identification with Moses was voiced when he compared Jung to a Joshua who would take possession of the promised land of psychiatry while he, Freud, the Moses, was destined to glimpse it only from afar. The figure of Moses, Freud confided in a colleague in 1935, had haunted him all his life. He told another colleague, 'Leave me alone with Moses . . . the man pursues me incessantly.'[4]

Moses was one of the leaders and prophets who founded a new religion. The image of the prophet who was without honour in his own country, yet would finally prevail and be universally accepted, was part of Freud's vision. Freud's wish to lead his people out of psychological bondage by the new revelation of psychoanalysis necessitated the destruction of the religion of the fathers. His interest in Moses culminated in the book *Moses and Monotheism* (1939), where Freud made a final attempt to resolve his ambivalent identification with the figure of Moses and through him the unfinished business in his relationship with his own father and his Jewish inheritance.[5]

Freud, through all his personal struggles and professional experience, created a language to describe our minds, and has become for us 'a whole climate of opinion'[6] of which the growth of therapy and counselling is a part. His ideas about the unconscious, inner conflict, the meaningfulness of apparently meaningless activity, the displacement and transference of feelings, psychosexual development and the centrality of early relations and experiences, are the bedrock of most interpersonal schools of therapy. Against the conventional assumption that each person knows his or her own self best, Freud thought that each is furthest from their own self and needs to journey through experience in search of it. He wrote, 'Turn your eyes inward, look into your own depths, learn first to know yourself!'[7]

Taking on the psychoanalytic idea that there are different levels to our thinking can itself be a helpful guide to making sense of a troubled childhood, and unlocking the door to spiritual recovery. The parting of the Red Sea can be seen as a metaphor for the separation of the confusion between past and present, and our conscious and repressed unconscious feelings. If we embark on journeying home with someone to guide us, various dynamics inevitably emerge as we start to see ourselves through the relationship with another. When these dynamics emerge in the therapeutic relationship they not only help with the development of our thinking through the past, but also, I believe, start to free our thinking about our relationship with God.

Returning once again to St Bernard's degrees of love – it is at this point that we may be able to love or have compassion for ourselves and start to love God for what he gives us. Sometimes our love can begin to feel desperate and clinging, and we realise that we are not yet really accepting that we are changing.

Alan's story

As we saw in Chapter 3, Alan became very anxious when I had to cancel our meetings because of flu. In this way Alan had brought the expectations that he would be let down and abandoned right into our relationship. These expectations had originated in his early experiences when his mother had been too ill to care for him, and now, unconsciously, in the sense that he was not aware of what he was doing, he had transferred them onto me. When Alan could acknowledge and think about this transference onto me he felt huge relief. One of the suggestions I made when we discussed what had happened, and tried to sort out his distress, was that Alan might feel angry at the cancelled sessions, and angry with me for letting him down.

'Angry?' replied Alan incredulously, 'angry – why on earth would I be angry? I was worried about you.' It was some time before he could experience and then think about his mixed feelings. He was too used to anticipating abandonment and disaster to think about any anger at the experience, or acknowledge his own murderous rage at being let down. His being was geared up to protect and defend against experiences rather than understand them. In that sense Alan found thinking difficult: his instinct was to react to life.

Another aspect of our relationship was that Alan felt very dependent on me. In a sense any relationship that encourages confessions fosters dependence. This dependence is nothing to fear or be avoided – rather, it is something that, if it can be worked through, serves to meet an unresolved need and an earlier deprivation. Such dependence can also evoke both feelings and thoughts in the other person. For example, I sometimes felt trapped by Alan's need for consistent meetings, and his need that everything be kept the same. His unspoken demand that I remain healthy and always able to see him began to feel like a huge pressure. It was inevitable that I would let him down, and this we discussed. I also found it helpful sometimes to discuss what was happening with another colleague. This supervision partly released the intensity of the relationship, and allowed for new thinking to emerge.

The pressure was based partially on Alan's need to know that I held in my mind a coherent sense of his being. It was as if it felt vital for me to know about all the bits and pieces in his life and the way he behaved. In that sense, at least, he could feel integrated in my mind, although he felt so fragmented in his own thinking. Alan felt he was at the mercy of his anxiety and fear – feelings that seemed initially to spring out to deflate and destroy him in a random manner. Bit by bit we were able to make sense of his attacks – there was always a trigger, usually linked to repressed and unacknowledged anger. Gradually Alan found that if he could think about what he was feeling, and if he got to it in time, the symptom often was deflected, and certainly became less powerful. We spoke about the idea of 'joined-up thinking': Alan no longer needed to project onto me the 'thinking part of himself'. He saw me as the person who was supposed to know what was happening in his (Alan's) mind, and part of the freedom to think was helping him accept that capability in himself.

The problem for anyone trying to sort this out, either with someone or alone, is how to interrupt and break up the previous expectations, and accept that new and different outcomes are a possibility. When I had a holiday break this too became a time of high anxiety for Alan. He was worried about how he would cope without seeing me – what if a new symptom appeared and feelings overwhelmed him? What if something terrible happened to either of us, and we never met again? What if he, the adult Alan, was left feeling for ever like he had felt at eighteen months?

There were different ways we thought together about managing this. On several occasions we spoke on the telephone; over another break I sent him postcards, and he wrote to me. Alan also kept a diary and wrote down what he felt when the fears became too strong. Another way we tried to interrupt this terror was to encourage him to think of himself in parts. Rather than proving a fragmenting experience, Alan found great consolation in thinking about his 'young child part of himself' and the 'adult part of himself'. If he could separate out what was happening there was a possibility that he, as adult, could comfort and reassure the 'child part of himself' in a way that he had not experienced at the time of the actual traumatic events, nor subsequently.

Sometimes he could recognise that what he felt, especially about symptoms, had become ridiculous – as he said, 'I'm almost a caricature of myself, there are times when I really could laugh at myself, if I wasn't feeling so bad!' Alan could see what he was doing and almost take a step back from his behaviour. He found it helpful to think that the feelings he sometimes had were the feelings of that earlier time. I suggested that he remember to say to himself, 'This is how terrible I felt when I was little, when no one understood and I was not able to help myself by thinking about it.' The essential difference to hold on to was that now it was different. 'Now I can think and know what is happening, I can speak and describe it and I can get support if I need it.' Alan now had a great many more resources to deal with what was happening. He had words, he could write down what he felt, he could speak to his girlfriend and he could pray.

As the work with Alan developed, so did his use of prayer and meditation. It had moved from being a cry of desperation and fear to something regular and calmer. He found that at the end of the day he could go through what had happened, and how he had felt, as part of his prayer time with God. Alan found great comfort in the idea of being held in the 'everlasting arms of Jesus' and felt that this image helped enormously when his young child part of himself felt too much. Gradually he began to transfer his dependence on me to a dependence on Jesus Christ. He found enormous consolation in Jesus' words, 'I will not leave you orphaned; I am coming to you' (John 14:18), and in Psalm 27:10, 'If my father and mother forsake me, the Lord will take me up.' His religious practice was conducted in private at this time, as he did not feel he wanted to be part of a regular church congregation. Alan felt that his religion was born of desperation and essentially based on this broken child part of himself. Although he did not feel consciously ashamed, he thought that if he spoke to anyone in a church, his informal and needy approach to Jesus would be frowned on, or seen as deficient or immature by other Christians. This was also about the grown-up part of Alan who was sometimes embarrassed by his own depth of feeling and thought it soft and unmanly.

Getting lost in the wilderness

Being released from familiar ways of reacting and starting to think seriously about who we are, and the direction that we want to take, can be a frightening and daunting undertaking. It seems hardly surprising that the Hebrews released from the control of Pharaoh longed at times to return to what they knew and what felt predictable. The story in Exodus describes how the freed slaves proved unruly and at times mutinous. How like us! When good things happened, like the sea parting just when they needed it, they were thrilled, but after tough days in the desert with no sustenance they were ready to turn on their liberator and guide, and wished they were back in Egypt.

As is well documented, people released from actual captivity after a long time in prison find freedom difficult, and unless given help and support can be drawn back to what was familiar and destructive. Brian Keenan's last words of his account of his four and a half years as a hostage ring true also for those who have been psychically incarcerated, 'Freedom comes slowly at first.'[8] Another hostage, Terry Waite, wrote of his need to keep to his room following his release from the darkness of his cell: 'I need the solid assurance of four walls to contain me, a room to give a shape to the space which threatens to swallow me in the ever-present darkness . . . Coming out of captivity can be likened to coming up from the sea bed: come up too quickly and the diver suffers the bends.' He continues in his 1994 postscript, 'There is still a long, long way to travel and I shall press on. God has been good to me, and to those whom I love. "Each venture", said Eliot "is a new beginning." Indeed it is: in mortal life and in that which we call death.'[9]

In the narrative of the journey through the wilderness, we read the account of the creation of the golden calf by the Hebrews, as a tangible god to be worshipped. Is there an equivalent idolatry in our personal journeying home? One 'golden calf' is the sort of clinging devotion that excludes thinking. Another 'golden calf' could be seen as the attraction to take on the thinking of another person in the form of imitation or identification, rather than to allow for the emergence of one's own thinking. This is a form of false thinking, a sort of stuck-on thinking that we can absorb as a way of avoiding any feelings of emptiness or uncertainty within ourselves. After all, in leaving behind an old way of thinking, we may be frightened that there is nothing left inside us. Suppose I am just empty inside? At least my preoccupation with misery gives me an identity – makes me real. It is a temptation to fill that emptiness with something that seems instantly attractive. I think that is why self-help books that promise instant improvement or courses that offer immediate relief and even enlightenment attract so many. It may partially explain why the Christian message of the way of the cross is unpopular. No guaranteed or tangible gratification and satisfaction in this lifetime seems contained in that way. We are required to open ourselves, and our minds, to something unknown and unfamiliar, and place our trust in an invisible guide.

Kirsty's story – learning to think about the past

Kirsty needed to acquire a language and a way of thinking, and we began to do that by mapping her past out on paper. On this sheet, Kirsty drew a large tree of life and, beginning at the roots, documented various incidents, house and school moves, and some good times that she could remember. With each notch on the tree Kirsty thought about what she had felt, and what she now thought about that time. Along the branches Kirsty documented feelings that linked to each experience and the 'fruits' of these feelings. She thought that some of the 'fruits' were bad and some were 'good', but most contained a mixture of 'good' and 'bad' outcomes. Kirsty worked on her tree both in the time with me and on her own at home. She also changed her mind about what she thought, so several months after the first tree she drew another tree which sometimes had different fruits, and this documented the changes in her thinking that had taken place. At one point Kirsty used family photographs to build up a collage of the past; another time she arranged the photos in a pattern to represent her relationship with each person from her family and group of friends. This, she found, helped her to gain a better perspective on her relationships.

Kirsty found the very process of documenting her past helpful. It gave her a chance to see the history of her child-hood and adolescence in sequence, and understand how her views had developed from her experiences. She found that she began to remember more and more about her childhood, and that even memories about different places she had lived, and different schools she had attended, helped explain things for her. For example, Kirsty had left school without any qualifications and this meant she often felt intellectually inadequate. In fact part of her difficulty in speaking was that she didn't believe that she knew how to think. As she gradually remembered all the schools she had gone to, she also remembered how sometimes she was ahead of the new class and had already done the work, and sometimes behind and so missed out completely. She had also been preoccupied by the unhappiness at home and found it hard to concentrate at school. As she understood these experiences, and thought about them, Kirsty remembered incidents both at school and at work, some that involved humiliation but others where she was praised. This discovery freed up her image of herself as 'just stupid'. She felt more compassionate about her school career, and began to see herself as intellectually thwarted rather than lacking. This changed self-image resulted in Kirsty eventually enrolling on an art course, which she enjoyed and which helped her further explore her emotions and gain self-confidence.

As Kirsty remembered certain events she also found that occasionally she could recapture the feeling that she had had at the time – it was a memory bound by time and space. Sometime towards the end of our work together Kirsty told me of a memory of an event when she was about seven years old. This was not a traumatic memory, rather a moment in time, and it became an important symbol in Kirsty's struggle to free herself from the past. In the memory, she had left her parents rowing in the kitchen, and had gone outside into the yard that ran alongside the house. Kirsty had leant against the outside wall of the house, and remembered feeling the rough bricks warm against her fingers and back. The sun was on her face. Above her an aeroplane rose, droning, in the blue sky, behind her the voices of her parents were less distinct, and Kirsty knew at that moment, aged seven, that she was apart from them and had her own existence.

Christopher Bollas, a psychoanalyst, calls these experiences an historic set, 'a holding space in memory, which stores the child's experience of being himself at that time in his world'. He feels this natural act and conservative process is essential to living, 'that stores the essence of being, to give to the construction of his psyche (his internal world) an historic depth, a matrix of material that bears the trace of the journey taken by the true self'.[10] Kirsty's historical set conserved her self-experience, and in the remembering of that moment Kirsty, as an adult, could again draw on that insight. The prior self became an important present self-experience. Christopher Bollas notes that often objects, such as the feel of the brick wall for Kirsty, become part of the way of thinking about one's life at the time.

Kirsty's experience with her parents had left her with a limited ability to conceptualise both what she thought in her own mind, and what she thought might be going on in the mind of another person. As Kirsty herself realised, when she was growing up a great deal of what went on around her was crude, demanding and aggressive. In that sense the conditions for developing reflective and thoughtful behaviour did not exist. In her father she saw responses based on impulse, and immediate and often uncontrollable feeling. When he was angry he shouted, when he was frustrated he lashed out. In her mother she saw weary and resigned responses. When it all became too much her mother became cold, silent and withdrawn.

To change this pattern from the past and develop the ability to think about her own feelings and other people's Kirsty needed a chance to practise and sometimes, even, model her own thoughts from hearing how other people were thinking. She often used experiences from television or films to explore her own feelings about something, or would tell me about terrible events that had happened to others and describe how they said they felt. At the beginning of our contact, when Kirsty would say she didn't have a clue about what she felt, I might present her with different options – did she feel sad or angry about something, or were there confused feelings around?

One example of this was when Kirsty told me that her daughter had been offered a place at college to train as a nurse. This was what both Kirsty and her daughter wanted, but something did not feel right. Kirsty had been cross and could not understand why. As we unravelled all the mixed feelings Kirsty was able to pinpoint both her feelings of pride and her feelings of resentment and loss. Her daughter had opportunities that she, Kirsty, had not had, and this gave rise to both pleasure and pain as she thought about this in comparison with her own deprivation.

The ability to accept what another person might be thinking first of all involves being able to sort through what we believe and what we want. We then need to be able to keep those as our own thoughts, rather than sharing them or experiencing the associated feeling through our behaviour. What does this mean? Again this is about seeing other people as separate and sometimes different from the way we are, and adjusting the way we relate and behave with them. In other words, feelings are owned for oneself, and acknowledged in another, without having to be acted on or expressed. Kirsty found that she no longer had to drink heavily in response to upsetting events; on the whole she now felt it was possible to manage and control the emotional fallout by thinking about it. She could think that I might have a different view of something from her, and yet not feel let down, or that she had to think the same as me. If we thought differently it didn't mean that we liked each other any less or had to hurt the other until we agreed.

In terms of her relationship with her father, Kirsty seemed, over time, to have become able to recognise how her father had been, and take responsibility for how he had affected her. She was able to acknowledge that he had been a bully, an unpredictable drinker with a violent temper, and also that he in turn at times had felt frustrated and ashamed at his behaviour. Towards the end of his life, when he had stopped drinking, he had tried to make amends towards his wife. He had been devastated by her sudden death, and he only lived a few months longer. Kirsty needed time to assimilate and come to terms with all this, and she found it both a relief and painful to talk and think about. This discovery of her own freedom to think resulted in a change in the mental pictures of her parents, and the part that they had both played in their married relationship with each other and with her.

The prodigal child

In the story of the prodigal son we read about the young man's release from his state of oppression, and his freedom to begin to think in verses 17–20.

> 'But when he came to himself he said, "How many of my father's hired hands have bread enough and to spare, but here I am dying of hunger! I will get up and go to my father and I will say to him, 'Father, I have sinned against heaven and before you; I am no longer worthy to be called your son; treat me like one of your hired hands.' " '

The New English Bible version uses the expression 'then he came to his senses' (v. 17). This breakthrough and awareness of his current predicament conveys the break from the state of oppression, and the beginning of his ability to think for himself, rather than the sort of not-thinking or reactive behaviour described in the first part of the story. Sadly his thinking then becomes formulaic, and he plans how he will approach his father, and placate and manipulate his way back into his home.

We all know about those sudden moments of awareness and realisation. 'The penny drops', 'it all makes sense', we suddenly 'see it all clearly'. These are much valued moments of 'coming to one's senses' or of 'coming to oneself'. The

Children's Bible version uses a different expression in the story: 'he suddenly broke down'. Perhaps a rather well-worn therapeutic expression is that 'it is not a breakdown, rather a breakthrough', but there is something truthful in that. If we cannot go on with how things are, or if we are forced to stop the way we live our life through illness, exhaustion or mental collapse, this can be the reason to break away from past thinking. In other words, in order to feel better again we see that something has to give and something has to change. When we suddenly become aware of something we see it differently – 'it doesn't have to be like this.'

Thoughts and emotions are certainly interwoven. We cannot think without emotion, even if it remains well hidden. We may have difficulty in knowing what we are thinking and feeling but it seems that mixed up in the raw sensations of both love and hate are subtle judgements and a need to understand what is happening inside us. Wilfred Bion, a psychoanalyst and philosopher, wrote about the development of thought from raw primitive emotion. He believed there was a hierarchy of thought, and expressed it using the model of infancy in the context of the infant in pain (we can also substitute here the adult's mind) searching for and being found by the mother's breast (we can substitute here the therapist's mind). In other words, he describes how there are embryonic thoughts seeking a container – thoughts seeking a thinker. If pain can be held by another, there is a possibility that they can be transformed sufficiently to be returned to the person in a more manageable form.

How can we understand this? Imagine feeling very confused and uncertain, full of unresolved anxieties and concerns, and yet unable to make any clear sense of them or understand why the anxiety seems so strong. If we can find the right person there is tremendous relief in having the opportunity to express all this, even if it feels incoherent, and to realise that the other person can listen and think about what one is saying. Even greater relief comes from the other person helping us sort the anxieties into coherent meaning once we have calmed down, and are able to hear what is being said. When Wilfred Bion linked this experience of gaining relief from someone else's capacity to think about what we are feeling back to being a baby, he was thinking in this way. The tiny baby is overwhelmed by sensations of hunger and discomfort, and yet cannot find relief. Suddenly the mother arrives and, realising the problem, feeds the baby. The pain then goes, and the baby is full and experiences bliss. At an innate, instinctual level the baby was searching for that experience of being fed by a mother who could understand what was needed.

Wilfred Bion found it useful to separate the idea of thoughts from the apparatus for thinking the thoughts. His idea that there are already thoughts that are 'awaiting' a thinker implies that the individual has to develop an apparatus for thinking so that these thoughts can be made manifest by thinking them. To begin with there are physical sensations which we obviously continue to experience throughout life but, unlike babies, we usually can know what we need. Sometimes if the experience is particularly strong, or in strange circumstances, it can take us back to raw, primitive emotion, for example, the same sensations felt by the hungry baby longing for the mother's breast would have been felt by the adult prodigal son when he was starving, 'and no one gave him anything'. Sometimes we can feel very raw and vulnerable when we feel excluded, misunderstood and hungry for affection and acceptance by someone.

If we are not able to think about the painful experience, then we push out all the bad feelings onto someone or something else, and we then feel under attack from that person or situation. So, for example, the mother who does not respond to the hungry baby becomes 'bad', and in the story of the prodigal son, the absent father who feeds his servants so well but not the son becomes a tyrant who has to be placated in the mind of the hungry son. If we are excluded and rejected it's all the fault of the other person and we want to hurt them as we too have been hurt. If we do not develop our thinking the world becomes an unsafe and paranoid-making place. If we do develop our thinking, then the pain of all these different experiences becomes mitigated through our thoughts. In other words the baby retains a mental image of the mother that sustains him or her through the absence, and the prodigal son possesses the father in thought and remembers his kindness. 'The foundation of thought lies in an absence. The thought itself has a constructive function; it creates the basic elements of experience into a meaningful pattern ... transforms persecutory ideation into a meaningful pattern.'[11] So thinking involves a move from a formless state – things just are that chaotic way (the prodigal son found himself feeding pigs) – to a state where coherence becomes manifest and a new understanding realised (the prodigal son came to his senses).

It is around the idea of thinking that some of the differences between therapy and religion can be seen. The process of therapy is partly about building the ability to self-analyse – in other words to think through our actions, feelings and responses. This is clearly crucial in the recovery from childhood trauma. However, sometimes when we have developed the ability to think about things, that very thinking can become formalised and rigid. It can turn from a freedom to think to a different shade of restrictive or prescriptive thinking. In other words, we may be able to integrate our experiences of painful childhood experiences, but find ourselves again limiting our thinking and beliefs.

Religion offers something different. It potentially offers an opportunity to lay aside our formalised thinking about how we should be and what we should do in the world. It offers the idea of stopping always thinking about ourselves, and allowing our thoughts to be guided by the Spirit through worship and prayer. It also offers the possibility of letting go of our self-importance, and thinking with a different perspective. The idea of thoughts waiting for a thinker can be carried into belief in God. Surely God is a constant presence surrounding us – if only we could turn and notice? Part of us longs for God and to have thoughts about him; and the thinker who can help us with that is Jesus Christ, and our relationship with Christ radically changes everything. If we can begin to trust Jesus Christ, who knows what we need before we do, if we can allow him to feed us, then there is the promise of bliss.

In the next two chapters we turn to the part played by imagination and belief in our recovery. Finding this can affect and transform our thinking and belief and allow us to return to an authentic relationship with God.

CHAPTER SIX

State of estrangement

IN THE NEXT two chapters we explore a third story that we can use on our journeying home. In Chapters 2 and 3 we looked at a way of journeying through guilt to forgiveness and at the physical expression of childhood trauma as mainly demonstrated through the body and body image. The last two chapters discussed the journey through a state of oppression towards liberation and centred on mental expression in the mind, and the effect on our thinking. In this chapter we look at the effect of the past on our spirit and in our spiritual life. The biblical story for this route on our journeying is one that describes a state of estrangement or exile, and then the return home.

What happens to our creativity, our capacity to play and fantasise if we have suffered as children? Can we play 'let's pretend' and let our imagination be free? Can we believe and hope in something better for ourselves and for others? Can we truly believe in something different from what we have already experienced, and so move on, having integrated the traumatic past? If we have the chance, can we believe in a loving God, or do we inevitably distort any idea of God?

In this chapter, we turn to the first half of the story and acknowledge the state of estrangement and exile where we may find ourselves. If we have had a tough and painful time during childhood it may be that experiences have blunted our spirit and our ability to play and imagine. In the next chapter the solution to return home and restore relationship is explored. If our capacity to believe can be restored then we have a choice whether or not to respond to God's generous invitation and belong to the family of faith. It is only when we recognise and are in many ways released from the obstacles of the past, those in body, mind and spirit that separate us from or distort our relationship with God, that we are then free to open ourselves and make that choice in an authentic way.

The story of exile and return

This is based on the historical experience in 587 BCE of the conquest of Jerusalem by Babylon. The accounts and the visions of the prophets Jeremiah and Ezekiel describe God's messages of what had gone wrong, and their hope for the future. In the biblical account some of the Jewish survivors were taken into exile in Babylon some eight hundred miles away, and lived as refugees. The exile ended about fifty years later when the Persians in turn conquered the Babylonian empire, and the refugees were allowed to return to their homeland.

In Psalm 137 the lament is initially one of grief and loss:

By the rivers of Babylon –
there we sat down and there we wept
    when we remembered Zion.

The psalm then moves into words of anger and revenge. As Trevor Dennis wryly notes, it is not the self-curse of the middle section of the psalm that so troubles us, but the twisted beatitudes of the final verses (7–9).

Remember, O Lord, against the Edomites
    the day of Jerusalem's fall,
how they said, 'Tear it down! Tear it down!
    Down to its foundations!'
O daughter Babylon, you devastator!
    Happy shall they be who pay you back

103

what you have done to us!
Happy shall they be who take your little ones
and dash them against the rock!

Trevor Dennis writes, 'They turn the language of blessing into curse, and leave us with the image of babies taken by the heels and swung against hard rock. Quickly we put brackets around those verses and leave them unsaid.'[1]

Once again we recognise the deep feelings of anger and outrage that are often part of our human experience. Such feelings can at times be overwhelming and need to be accepted and recognised rather than ignored, or hidden away as inappropriate or unpleasant. Better to speak of our resentment and bitterness than keep it bubbling away just under our surface consciousness where it can suddenly erupt and shock us and others. Paradoxically, accepting these violent and passionate feelings can be a way of finding our true self. It is part of regaining and restoring our sense of self – part of the process of acknowledgement and reconciliation within our inner world. In the context of healing the wounds from a troubled childhood, this first part is about estrangement from our true spiritual 'home', and it is about all the emotional after-effects we have about that separation.

What does this mean? There seem to be two relevant meanings in this part of our journeying. The first is that of a disconnection within ourselves – we become a stranger to our true self and our true potential. In other words we put our self in exile. We long for something that we can barely remember, something that we might have known a long time ago. In an earlier chapter I quoted Winston Smith in *1984* reflecting on 'a feeling that you had been cheated of something you had a right to', although, 'It was true that he had no memories of anything greatly different.'[2] We may not remember anything different, but deep inside us the longing for healing and for a sense of inner completion has not been extinguished.

Imagine what it is like to have grown up in a strict home

devoid of love and affection – in a regime of duty and respon-sibility. One day you are invited to tea by a school friend and in your friend's home you see how family life can be different. There is warmth and generosity of spirit, perhaps there is a cheerfulness or casualness that you are at first excluded from, but gradually feel drawn towards and accept. This brief experience gives a glimpse of what is possible – things do not always have to be the same, some families are different.

The second meaning that I shall focus on in this state of estrangement is to do with our capacity to believe and trust. The capacity to believe in something loving has gone or been corrupted. If we try to force ourselves to believe we can come up against a lack or failure in our imagination. My suggestion is that this capacity to believe in something 'greatly different' has been blunted, and we have placed ourselves in exile as a way of managing our painful childhood experience. Then the glimpse of something different – for example the way another family lives and relates – is too painful to contemplate. The misery of the not-having means that we have to deny our-selves that glimpse and so we make sure that we do not return to that warm house, and the friendship ends. It is beyond our imagination to believe that we too might be able to have that experience, and we do not want to be reminded of the painful recognition of our own deprivation.

Many stories in the Bible test our imagination and belief. One of them is the narrative about the prophet Ezekiel. He acted as an inspiration to the exiled Jewish refugees, and became a mediator between God and them. In the most famous of his visions, the Spirit of God takes the prophet to a bleak valley full of dry bones. A miracle takes place. God empowers Ezekiel to bring all the bones back to life. The first stage is physical, and as Ezekiel speaks to the bones they become fully formed human bodies. Next he calls for breath to enter them and they become fully alive. As Andrew Mein notes, the key word here is the Hebrew *ruah*, which can be translated 'spirit' or 'wind' as well as 'breath'.[3] In their exile the people have reached the depths of desolation: 'Our bones are dried up, and our hope is lost; we are cut off completely.' In the place of estrangement all hope has gone, and there is a profound disconnection. Ezekiel's vision is that God will take them home and bring them back to life.

In a sense when we are divorced from our spiritual life we are incomplete. We may be physically assured and intellectually aware, but part of us has been banished. In that sense we are like the dry bones: we await the breath of life to revive us and bring us fully alive.

Estranged from our true self

The paediatrician and psychoanalyst Donald Winnicott also wrote, like Thomas Merton, about the true self and the illusory and false self (he used capitals, but I shall keep to the lower case except when I directly quote him). Although he is writing from a developmental and psychoanalytic perspective, there are important overlaps with the spiritual perspective put forward by Thomas Merton. For Donald Winnicott the true self was linked to the experience of aliveness, it was what for each person gives the feeling of real, and can only be found by each person for him- or herself. The function of the false self, he felt, is to hide and protect the true self from destruction and annihilation, and it develops initially in response to a mother or mothering person who is unable to respond in a good-enough way to the infant's spontaneous gestures and needs. Instead the mother substitutes her own gesture and interpretation of what is happening, which is given sense and so accepted through the compliance of the infant.

What does that really mean? Imagine a situation where the hungry baby described in the previous chapter is crying, but instead of going to feed him, the mother decides that the baby needs to be left for longer. In her mind it is too soon, and anyway babies need to learn to wait. That's what has happened to her all her life, and in her mind it does no harm – in fact it's a good thing. Over time the baby will adjust to her attitude and institute a way of denying his discomfort to fit with mother's view of the world. In this sort of situation the infant lives and develops, but in a false way.

Remember Jim, as a small boy, waiting for his unreliable father to appear for a visit. Part of his need to keep his father good is fuelled by his need to avoid his mother's anger about the situation. If Jim turned to his mother for comfort, all he would hear is a tirade against her faithless and abandoning husband. Jim has learnt to keep his pain to himself. Over time, as the situation is repeated, Jim learns to accept his mother's view of his father. He fits in with her, rather than risk further pain and conflict. In childhood our compliant false self reacts to what happens and seems to accept the parental demands, although it is worth noting that there are also always signs of protest. In other words the anger and upset does not, as we realise, completely disappear. Rather the emotional fallout tends to reappear in a different form later in our adolescence or adulthood.

Donald Winnicott writes, 'Through this False Self the infant builds up a false set of relationships, and by means of intro-jections even attains a show of being real, so that the child may grow up to be just like mother, nurse, aunt, or brother, or whoever at the time dominates the scene ... Compliance is then the main feature, with imitation as a speciality.'[4] What are the effects of all this? One major outcome is that if we are compliant and merely fit with what others want from us, then we lack creativity and our imagination is restricted. Further-more, in the context of the development of our spiritual life, if we then assume that such compliance is a quality in our relationship with God we are not only repeating our earlier experiences, but also distorting and deadening the relation-ship. It is the opposite of the breath of life – rather, it is the kiss of death. This compliance was one aspect of Alan's difficulties as he grew up; compliant behaviour was

107

demanded of Kirsty, and both their experiences are explored further in this chapter.

There are clearly different degrees of false self-organisation that range from a state where our true self is kept completely hidden (totally in exile) to a state where our false self searches for conditions for our true self to come into its own (returning home). In other words, it can range from a state where we mostly believe that we are the false self, with just the faintest whisper of the true self in hiding, to the search by the false self for some help to allow the true self within us a chance to emerge. We all have a measure of false self about us. It is the 'best behaviour' we put on in certain company, but usually we know what we are doing. If we are healthy, then we can if we need override this polite false self, and allow the true self to speak. For example, if we need to say what we really feel and think about some situation, then we are able to allow our true self to speak whatever the setting and the company.

Donald Winnicott quotes a patient of his, who previously had had much futile analytic treatment on the basis of a false self that co-operated vigorously with an earlier analyst who had thought this was the patient's whole self. The person told Winnicott after the treatment with Donald Winnicott was over, 'The only time I felt hope was when you told me that you could see no hope, and you continued with the analysis.'[5] In the same way even if we feel hopeless in our attempts to seek and return to God, we need to keep part of ourselves open. If we are to have a meaningful and authentic relationship with God then we need to begin to try to reveal our true self both to ourselves and to God in our prayer life. We need to ask for his help in uncovering who we really are.

Alan's story – estranged through compliance

After Alan's initial separation trauma at eighteen months, he had apparently become a nervous and unsettled toddler. He recollected being told that he had been 'a bag of nerves'.

Subsequent illnesses in his mother had meant further separations, and Alan remembered always feeling watchful towards her and worrying about how she was feeling. As well as her ill health, and perhaps partly because of it, Alan described his mother as rather complaining, sometimes adopting a martyred approach in the family. Alan felt that his brother and his father had taken refuge in a shared interest in sport, which meant they were away from home a great deal, and leaving him, the younger son, as companion and confidant to his mother. His anxiety about her, combined with the fear of his own destructive impulses and fantasies about her, made him protective towards her, and as he grew up he became increasingly compliant. Using Donald Winnicott's terms one might say that Alan developed a false self that fitted with his mother's needs and left his own unfulfilled.

Alan remembered having an imaginary friend when he was about four and five – this was Harry D.D. Alan had later understood that this stood for 'dare devil', a term he had not really understood at the time, but he had felt was to do with being naughty. Harry D.D. went everywhere with Alan and often started 'to do things' that the well-behaved Alan would not have dreamt of, such as once taking money from his brother and wanting to run away. In this way Alan, through Harry D.D., had kept part of himself alive and rebellious, and outside the compliant good-boy frame put in place by the family.

In the course of our work together Alan often talked about his dreams. Dreams are usually an interesting and helpful way of talking and thinking about what is going on underneath our conscious awareness. Often there is little need for intricate dream work to unravel the meaning, and sometimes we can clearly see what is happening in our inner world, and how it is represented, through remembering our dreams. The night after our first meeting, Alan had dreamt that he and I were riding together in a brightly coloured toy car up a long, steep hill. It reminded him of a picture in a storybook he had read as a small child. On one side there was a deep forest with dark fir trees, but on the other side of the road the view was clear. We understood that this was a dream about the therapeutic work that needed to happen, and that although there was a long path to cover based on his childhood experiences, the dark and the light seemed evenly balanced, and I was with him on the journey.

The setting for a later dream that encapsulated Alan's struggle to free himself from his false self, in order to allow the true self to emerge, took place in the house he had lived in for most of his childhood. In the dream Alan's mother was in the kitchen complaining and Alan's father and brother in the dining room waiting to eat. Alan saw himself in the dream as a cardboard figure, like the large cut-out figures used for advertising promotions. He was one-dimensional, flattened and not real. He looked neatly dressed and smiling, and was rushing into the kitchen to help his mother. This was a dream that needed little interpretation – it could be easily read and understood. Alan saw that all along, deep inside himself, he had known about this false self. It had acted as a care-taking self to protect him from further painful upset, avoid angry feelings and so make sure that everything remained safe.

Alan's imagination was certainly present; sometimes it worked overtime, especially when anticipating disasters, but it was totally controlled by the need to be compliant and patterned by past experiences. He longed to break free from this to allow for different and more creative possibilities. Some time after we had stopped our regular meetings, and Alan was feeling stronger and clearer about himself and what had happened to him as a child, this tendency to be compliant in relationships involving 'authority' or 'parental' figures began to emerge again in his developing dependence on Jesus Christ. We met up to discuss this and Alan described how he had evolved a ritual for his evening prayers. This he liked and stuck to, but then felt devastated if he had to miss the routine. This would mean that the next night Alan would add extra time and extra prayers praising Christ – not because he wanted to, but because he felt he should. Once again Alan had created a figure that needed to be placated, and with whom there then seemed little creative choice. He felt that this was what was wanted, and he should fit with these demands. Alan realised that there was some confusion in his mind about being obedient and saying prayers, and whether or not he was just being compliant. He also sometimes worried in case his praising God was another form of appeasement. At this stage it seemed as if it would be helpful for Alan to discuss his worries within a religious rather than a therapeutic context, and Alan left to think through various possibilities.

The capacity to believe

In the analysis of the true self, you may remember that Donald Winnicott spoke of a sense of aliveness – being and feeling real. Sometimes if a child has experienced abuse, brutality or neglect, a great part of their imagination can become blunted, dulled or even lost. Why is this? Actual physical events and traumas seem to extinguish the opportunity for fantasy. For example, if sexual abuse has taken place there is no room left for sexual fantasy, for forbidden and repressed musings about possible sexual experiences, or even about loving and longing for physical tenderness. It is as if the actual, concrete nature of the trauma dominates. There is no room for 'what if' or 'maybe'. Trauma, in other words, is hard to translate into metaphor. It remains literal. It has happened, and nothing can be the same again.

People who have been exposed to horrifying and de-humanising conditions, especially over a period of time, limit their behaviour to the primary needs of self-preservation; it becomes unambiguous, with little room for the use of fantasy and for 'as if' or spontaneous feeling. The task is to survive and get through. One person I met spoke of having to just 'get through' to eighteen when she knew that she could leave home. Sometimes the only way to survive is to resort to violence and angry outbursts. If there is no other outlet for such strong aggression, then the only option is to turn against one's own body and person. Some of us cannot think about rage, but need to express it in any way we can.

In other words, the capacity for understanding metaphor and using the imagination, and the capacity to believe in something different are both severely impaired by a troubled childhood. Sometimes also the ability to remember dreams is partially or wholly restricted. In his work on child abuse Leonard Shengold quotes Randall Jarrell on children who had grown up in what Jarrell describes as 'one of God's concentration camps'. He is referring here to families and homes where brutality, totalitarianism, abuse or neglect was the norm. The route out of such dehumanising experiences is the way we have been exploring through this book. This is the conscious development of feeling – both for oneself and for another, when previous experience has led to the expectation that opening oneself to feeling leads to feeling torment.[6]

Part of the development of the capacity to believe, lies, I think, in gradually letting go of the attachment to the parent or adult who was responsible for the childhood suffering. This involves bringing to conscious awareness and understanding the deep dependency, and the internal need to hold on to the neglectful or abusing parent figure in the inner world. This often takes the form of identification, as it did for both Kirsty (taking on her father's aggression) and Alan (taking on his mother's illnesses and needs). A crucial struggle has to take place for those of us who have suffered and been troubled as children. The adult struggle is to let go and appreciate that we can live without the mother, or father, or whoever was central to the traumatic experience.

As we have previously considered, if the dependence moves to the therapist, or pastoral worker, then these issues can be thought about in the relationship, and feelings of shame, guilt and anger tolerated within the therapeutic relationship. This is the idea of the transference, where all the strong feelings that have been kept down from the past can be explored. Destruction does not need to take place if destructive fantasies can be spoken about. Talking about murderous rage – including smashing babies against rocks – can release the angry tension and defuse dangerous impulses.

This is what is so encouraging about the person who wrote Psalm 137. It demonstrates a relationship between the person writing the psalm and God that is authentic and open, and so able to withstand such vicious expressions of rage and anger. The writer was not afraid to voice these feelings and fantasies in lamenting the misery of exile. In a similar way the experience of sharing these deep emotions in a therapeutic relationship can allow for such emotions to be contained. Fantasising, daydreaming and dreaming can all provide ways for the eventual transformation of passionate emotions into a growing capacity for concern and appreciation of the other person. For example, for some people their rage can emerge through powerful dream images involving uncontrollable fires and destruction. It helps if we are able to write such dreams down or tell someone about them rather than just ignore or deny them.

The capacity to believe in change, for example that things might be different; that all relationships are not the same; in the possibility of healing; in the existence of God – such a capacity requires some kind of trust and faith. Trust and faith have to be experienced in order to be believed in. The word 'capacity' derives from the Latin *capere* meaning 'to hold' or 'to contain' and is related to the adjective *capax*, which means roomy or capacious. It also links to 'capable' and the idea of the ability or the potential to do things. The capacity to believe may be something we are potentially born with but, as we have recognised, it also needs to be nurtured over time in an appropriate environment.

In his exploration of this idea Donald Winnicott seems to

suggest that the development of that capacity must come before whatever it is that is eventually believed in. 'In other words, there can be no "believing in" without the child's first having developed the capacity for "belief in", an interior space in which to *put* beliefs. That requires the attainment of a certain depth, depth enough to recognise that there are things worth believing in at all.' He picked up the psycho-analytic stance that God is only a projection, but suggested that even so this might imply the existence of a God who created us with the capacity for having such a projection. Some sort of relationship is implied between the capacity to have the idea of God and its prior existence, which contains us. Donald Winnicott wrote, 'Have I got it in me to have the idea of God? – if not, then the idea of God is of no value to me (except superstitiously).'[7] In other words we need to have the ability and capacity to believe in God, before we make the choice of whether to respond to God.

Kirsty's story – regaining spontaneity

In playing, the child or adult is free to be creative and spon-taneous. 'Let's pretend' functions as an imaginative improvisation deeply buried in metaphor. Kirsty did remember playing as a child with her brothers, but often the games were furtive and took place at snatched times when her father was away. If the children were playing when their father came in they stood frozen and silent, and gradually the games stopped altogether. One of the games that Kirsty recalled playing over and over again with her younger brother involved the two of them punishing and hurting a Barbie doll and a Ken doll. They would follow the same grim routine in the game, partially replicating the domestic violence they had witnessed. In this way their childhood trauma was barely disguised with metaphor. Both in her play and in her thinking Kirsty, as a child, could not move far enough away from her experiences to afford her any relief that she might have expected from playing. In other words she was stuck in replicating the real events. What had happened on the outside had become firmly established in her inside. Traditionally play is seen as a way of mastering experiences in childhood, but this game would have had to be played for years before much relief would have come. In some ways it also created new fear on top of what was there already, as Kirsty and her brother frightened themselves by devising, in their anger and aggression, possible new tortures and cruelties for the luckless Barbie and Ken.

When her father was at home the atmosphere became tense, and the children were watchful. Kirsty remembered a mealtime when her youngest brother began to hiccup, and Kirsty and her other brother started to laugh. Her father told them to stop laughing, but they could not obey. Kirsty said, 'I knew I had to stop but I couldn't, the giggling happened despite me.' Both she and her brother were hit across the head and sent to their rooms. The house was dominated by the threat and anticipation of violence, and by her father's moods. As the family moved around from posting to posting it was hard for Kirsty to establish close girlfriends, but she did go out to birthday parties and round to tea at other girls' houses, and told me that she would fantasise about what it would be like to live with different parents.

As our work progressed Kirsty felt she could trust me more, and also she developed faith in the process of talking things through. As it became possible for her to recall large parts of her childhood, she used her art classes as a way of ridding herself of some vivid mental pictures involving the domestic violence. One picture of her mother's bruised face she brought to show me. Kirsty felt by getting such mental pictures down on paper she might free herself from their power. In her mind and visual memory of her mother's injuries, they were often sharply clear as if seen in higher-intensity light, and she surprised herself by remembering tiny details. Kirsty also painted a recurring dream from childhood based on being trapped in a house and trying to close the door shut against a burglar, or bad man, threatening to break in. In the dream, as Kirsty bolted one door, she turned to find another had opened, or she had forgotten about shutting the window. As a child this had been a terrifying nightmare. As she painted the dream, Kirsty said that she now appreciated her real fear as a child of this violent and unpredictable father who threatened her sense of childhood invincibility, and left her with a waking dread of a limited future.

Kirsty's work in the art classes still seemed to be locked in the past and rather repetitive. However, a breakthrough came when a woman sculptor came to lead a session. Unlike the scene with the visiting facilitator of the relaxation class, Kirsty immediately took to this woman. She seemed ordinary to Kirsty – in fact she described her as rather dowdy and unassuming, but very warm and approachable. She did not threaten Kirsty. The class was made up of women of all ages, and the sculptor brought in large quantities of damp clay. To help the women relax and feel free to be creative she encouraged them, in the first part of the class, to take large dollops of the clay and hurl them on to the board on the floor. Kirsty told me that initially she had felt terribly self-conscious, as did the others, and they had rather apologetically dropped pieces from their hands. Then the leader took some clay and as she hurled pieces of clay down with all her might she yelled and leapt. Immediately, as if a switch had been turned, the whole group followed her example. Kirsty described it as the most exhilarating experience of her life. She had felt utterly free, very excited, and found herself laughing and crying, shouting and yelling. Then the group used the clay individually to create shapes that they felt might represent themselves. Kirsty's looked rather like a conch shell, with an open interior, and was beautifully decorated. As she had moulded the clay, she had recited to herself, 'I am who I am, I am alive, I am me', and she had created a beautiful shape. Kirsty was starting to believe in her self, beginning to under-

116

stand that she had survived her experiences, and starting to trust that things could be different for her.

The prodigal child – saying 'no' to relationship

The state of estrangement in the story of the prodigal son lasts until the moment that he is held and embraced by his father. However, the part of the story that encapsulates this place of spiritual separation is contained in the first part of verse 20. 'So he set off and went to his father. But while he was still far off . . .' In the context of this part of our journeying home, this fragment of verse contains a dilemma. It is as if from the depths of our despair about who we are and what we have done, and what has happened to us, we set off searching for the healing of our spirit. In the state of estrangement, part of us – centred in the spirit – remains still far off in terms of intimacy and relationship. There still can be a huge distance between the turning around and the arrival home. Henri Nouwen comments that this journey 'needs to be travelled wisely and with discipline', and that the return is full of ambiguities.[8] He comments on the confusion often present, and the self-serving repentance and thinking demonstrated in the story of the prodigal son as he prepares to return home. He still cannot trust the father to love, accept and forgive him, in the context of everything that has taken place.

Those who have suffered in childhood are very much those whom Jesus addresses and reaches for in the gospels. Using a contemporary slant on Scripture, we read that he reaches out to those who weep for what has happened to them; those who mourn the loss of a parent, or their own innocence; those who are hungry for love and acceptance; those who are captivated and stuck in a certain way of thinking or living; those who need medication or restraint to keep them in touch with reality or to prevent them harming themselves or others; those who have translated their pain into physical symptoms;

and the lost souls – the broken-hearted who can find no way to recover. However there is a dilemma here, for although the message is unambiguous, we may still not want or be able to trust it.

Perhaps one problem for those of us scarred by the past is the fear of the implications of any further dependence or submission. If we have learned to adjust and cope with the past, or if we have been through a painful process of coming to terms with what has happened, we may be reluctant to relinquish this new-found control and integration. The Christian is encouraged to become like a child again, to have a child's approach in his or her relationship with God. Jesus makes it clear that the way to God is the same as the way to a new childhood. 'Unless you change and become like children you will never enter the kingdom of heaven' (Matthew 18:3). Henri Nouwen writes of discovering the joys of the second childhood: 'Jesus does not ask me to remain a child but to become one. Becoming a child is living toward a second innocence: not the innocence of the newborn infant, but the innocence that is reached through conscious choices.'[9] For some people the fear and the danger is that known child-hood pain might be repeated, rather than the potential and promised experience of a new childhood – a second and different childhood.

One way of resolving this dilemma can be for people to become attracted and drawn to spiritual disciplines that involve no relationship, but instead foster a sense of control and detachment. Several people that I have worked with over many years, who longed for a spiritual dimension in their lives, found it helpful to practise yoga, or tai chi or other Eastern disciplines. These undoubtedly helped them regain a sense of control over their body, and can be especially thera-peutic for those who have been physically or sexually abused, or those who have experienced an emotionally intrusive relationship with a parent. Similarly people are drawn to meditation, particularly through practising Buddhist techniques, and use this as a way of managing unpleasant feelings and difficult thoughts. Eastern spiritual texts encourage disciplining and controlling the movement of the body and the breath, and clearing the mind as part of spiritual development.

One essential difference between such practices and becoming a Christian is that of relationship. Christianity involves a personal relationship with God. 'The discipline is that of becoming a child of God.'[10] To do this we need to take a leap of faith, make a conscious choice and believe in the possibility of restoration and reconciliation and that we have a home to return to. It is this second part of the story that is explored in the next chapter.

CHAPTER SEVEN

Returning home

Finally I am returning
to the place almost lost,
back by a circuitous route . . .

I am going home,
and on the road ahead
one is waiting and watching, softly
*   and tenderly welcoming*
with outstretched arms,
*   'ye who are weary, come home.'*[1]

IF OUR PROBLEM has been exile, and we have felt estranged from our true self and from the life of the spirit, then the solution is, of course, reconciliation and returning home.

> For thus said the Lord God, the Holy One of Israel:
> In returning and rest you shall be saved;
> in quietness and in trust shall be your strength.
>   (Isaiah 30:15)

Much of the second part of the book of Isaiah is an invitation and encouragement to take the return journey home. The poetic language of the unknown prophetic writer(s) describes a metaphoric route and a highway being built through the

wilderness, leading from exile in Babylon back to the Promised Land, and back home. Where is home? Home in this
story is the place where God is present – a place of spiritual
fulfilment. In exile we live outside this true home, but the
story includes the promise that if we start to make the journey
we will be both guided and helped by something 'more than
ourselves'.

> Strengthen the weak hands,
>> and make firm the feeble knees.
> Say to those who are of a fearful heart,
>> 'Be strong, do not fear!
> Here is your God.
>> He will come with vengeance,
> with terrible recompense.
>> He will come and save you.' . . .
>
> A highway shall be there,
>> and it shall be called the Holy Way . . .
> And the ransomed of the Lord shall return,
>> and come to Zion with singing;
> everlasting joy shall be upon their heads;
>> they shall obtain joy and gladness,
>> and sorrow and sighing shall flee away.
>>> (Isaiah 35:3–4, 8 and 10)

In this third part of our journeying home there has to be a
conscious letting go of the state of estrangement, a conscious
and developing awareness of becoming more open, and a
conscious working at the capacity to believe and trust in
different outcomes and relationships. This stage of relief and
recovery is that of conscious letting go. Here we may be able
to move to the second aspect of loving presented by St
Bernard of Clairvaux, and discussed in the introduction: 'We
love God for what he gives us.' Perhaps we can begin to
appreciate how we are changing and begin to have faith in
the process of healing from a troubled childhood. If we allow

ourselves to, we can feel thanks for new experiences and new possibilities. Perhaps we can experience the 'being given to' and the sense that we are not left alone and abandoned to what previously felt overwhelming.

This is about the capacity to believe that there is something more than ourselves, and that this 'more than ourselves' is something to which we can relate. It is about accepting that we have value and are lovable no matter how we have felt about ourselves in the past. It is about the process of receiving and accepting the love of God, if we can, and feeling gratitude for that relationship. If this is an experience that we can authentically allow ourselves, then we may also be able to 'love God for himself', rather than the distorted image we have projected, and in loving God for himself, we can move to the process of unconscious letting go from the state of estrangement. If we can leave the place of exile then we can be introduced into a new way of knowing ourselves and the world. This is the way of happening – where we can be open to difference and change, and we no longer need to hold on to the painful and the familiar just to feel safe.

Something more than myself

As discussed in the introduction to this book, there has been a history of suspicion between religion and psychotherapy. Most psychoanalytic ideas assume that religious experiences and religious relationships can only be understood in the context of distortions of our own mental activity and neurotic needs. In other words God becomes some sort of idealised projection, or part of infantile longings, or return to the womb, and so on. When we believe in God and live within that faith, such analytic thinking appears reductive and limited. While accepting that our image of God can be distorted by our own experiences, and in that sense is partially subjective, my belief is that beyond that there is something 'other', which can be experienced as both transcendent and immanent, and we are made in order to relate to, and connect with, this 'other'. Our defences against a belief in God often include the powerful defence against the possibility of a good relationship (or good object, in analytic jargon).

In his struggle with O'Brien and the Thought Police, Winston Smith in *1984* queries the idea that everything can be controlled by the mind and is a product only of that mental activity. 'And yet he knew, he *knew*, that he was in the right. The belief that nothing exists outside your own mind – surely there must be some way of demonstrating that it was false? Had it not been long ago exposed as a fallacy? There was even a name for it, which he had forgotten.' O'Brien, arch mind-reader, provides Smith with the missing word, 'solipsism', but denies that this is the case.[2]

Solipsism refers to a mindset where the self knows only its present state and is the only existent thing. Reality is subjective as it is a concern with the self at the expense of any relationship. We can experience solipsism when we deny feelings in another person – putting our self and our own needs right to the front of whatever is happening. Sadly this is often the state of mind of the adult who may be inflicting pain or abuse on the child. At that moment the adult cannot conceive what the child might be going through – the adult either cannot or will not think about what is happening. It links back to the idea explored earlier in the book about the development of the capacity of concern, and the acceptance and understanding that other people may think and behave differently from us.

Perhaps the state of collective solipsism describes those schools of thought, such as some psychotherapeutic trainings or some religious organisations, that refuse to entertain any other reality than their own dogma. In contrast, Paul Tournier offers a refreshing slant when he suggests that analytical technique can serve religion, and together they can achieve results of which they would be incapable separately.[3] Clearly by using aspects of analytic understanding and technique we can free ourselves from obstacles in the past that inhibit the development of mature and authentic religious belief.

When we are consumed by our own misery, anxiety or depression, it is hard to feel that anything can reach us, or that anything can feel as powerful as, or greater than, the distress we are experiencing. It is hard to think that there could be anything different or 'other' than the misery we feel. If we can reach the point of seeking some help, and turn to another person, or even to reading a book such as this one, we are admitting that there is some hope, that there may be something else, and that something different might be possible. Therapeutic and pastoral counselling, in whatever context it takes place, is an opportunity to know and be known by each other. Such a 'storm of emotional relating' forces us, as we have explored earlier in the book, to 'cope with feelings and subject them to thought'.[4] Gradually through the process of the therapeutic or pastoral relationship we can learn to understand and become aware of who we are, and how and why we behave the way we do, but also how we are with another person. If the therapy is going to work, then we need to learn to trust the other person not to harm us or distort what we are saying, and we need some faith that the process of talking about the past will help us. If we are using this book as a form of self-help then we are also beginning the process of knowing our self and gaining insight into how we react and respond to others.

We need to develop the capacity to believe, and we need these experiences of hope, trust and faith, in order to believe that our lives can be different. Therapy is one of the ways which can help us begin to understand that there is more than just our own consciousness, and that stuck in states of distress we are terribly limited in our knowledge of ourselves. We can start to overcome and integrate the suffering caused by a troubled childhood if we enter into, and acknowledge, the depths of our emotions.

However, I am suggesting that there is more than the

process of making the unconscious conscious, and also that there is more than a process of coming to terms with a troubled past. These very processes lead us to question a restrictive perspective based on what is literally seen and known, and the actual processes of seeing what lies below our immediate responses open up the possibility of spiritual belief and development. Psychotherapy is a relationship founded on pain and suffering. The relationship is seen as a way of alleviating such distress through insight into the unconscious, and is an awakening into what has made us the way we are, and how we might think about changing that. 'When this drama is fully engaged, it always leads to the great spiritual questions – Why are we here? Who are we, as humans? Why do we die? – but it cannot provide answers to these questions because it is not designed to function at such a universal level.'[5]

Jung thought that many patients coming for psychotherapy, especially those in the second half of their lives, primarily were searching for spiritual meaning. He called it a religious problem, though he understood that it might have nothing to do with going to church. The illness or distress might be the trigger for seeking help, but at a deeper level there was a longing to think seriously about the parameters of existence. In his poem 'Church Going' Philip Larkin writes of his visit to an empty church, 'a serious house on serious earth'. The poem includes the lines,

> Since someone will forever be surprising
> A hunger in himself to be more serious . . . [6]

Towards the end of his life, Jung summed up his reflections on the importance of acknowledging the unseen, spiritual life.

> The decisive question for man is, is he related to some-
> thing infinite or not? That is the telling question of his
> life. Only if we know that the thing that truly matters is
> the infinite can we avoid fixing our attention upon

futilities and upon all kinds of goals which are not of real importance ... In the final analysis we count for something only because of the essential we embody, and if we do not embody that, life is wasted.[7]

June Singer picks up that this question is also a decisive one for women, but that it is not necessarily *the* decisive question. In her experience, many women gain their sense of personal worth through loving relationships in this finite world.[8]

Perhaps it is rather a synthesis of these two slants, given that it is not until we can relate in an authentic and aware way to those we love and know, that we can relate without spiritual distortion to God. It is not until we have resolved our spiritual pathology that we are able to make the mature and clear choice to return to God. This choice involves a second birth and a second and different childhood.

The prodigal child – the father runs towards us

The last part of the story of the son's return home contains enormous implications for the healing of the spirit, and gives us encouragement because of the image of God portrayed through the figure of the father. We pick up the story in the second half of Luke 15:20: 'his father saw him and was filled with compassion; he ran and put his arms around him and kissed him.' Here at the heart of the story we are told of a parent – and it does seem here that God is portrayed as both a father and mother – who, waiting anxiously, and looking out, then runs to welcome the exile home. So what does this story tell us about the nature of God? We read that the parent is full of compassion, and wants his child back. This is not an angry, judging, or self-absorbed parent, but one who welcomes and understands. This is an image of unconditional love and compassion.

James Alison speaks of love as 'the coming towards us of what really and inalterably *is*, the regard which creates, while faith and hope are the given response from within us to what is; the given response which love calls forth, while we are "on the way". Faith and hope are a relaxing into our being uncovered, discovered, as someone loved. But they are a relaxing into love's discovery of us.' The one coming towards us is not coming to confront, but coming for us because 'he must actually have really known and liked us all along.'[9]

Henri Nouwen points out that, later in the story, the father also comes out to meet the elder dutiful son as he comes back from work, and pleads with him to join the celebration. Here there is no comparison between the children.

> Our God, who is both Father and Mother to us, does not compare. Never ... Here lies hidden the great call to conversion: to look not with the eyes of my own low self-esteem, but with the eyes of God's love ... [If] I am able to look at the world with the eyes of God's love and discover that God's vision is ... that of an all-giving and forgiving father who does not measure out his love to his children according to how well they behave, then I quickly see that my only true response can be deep gratitude.[10]

The whole story of the prodigal child is a story of grace. For many of us damaged by childhood troubles there is often no thought of the possibility of being in a state of grace. This means no thought of being loved and wanted for ourselves, or being acceptable within our own eyes or through the eyes of another. Yet as we have explored through the book, transitional, transformational or sacred moments can take place once we start to open ourselves to the possibility of change. Richard Holloway speaks of the moment of grace, 'this moment when we must run to meet ourselves as we trudge away from the country of self-hatred and say Yes to ourselves'.[11] This moment of grace can also be felt as the sheer joy and celebration of feeling accepted and alive. As Richard

Holloway points out, ultimately it is ourselves that we have to accept unconditionally.

After all, the story of the prodigal child that we have been following in each chapter also can be read as the journey to the moment of integration of our inner world. The culmination is the celebration of the uniting of three parts of our self as represented by the three characters in the story. One part is the angry, impulsive, selfish part, dominated by bodily pleasures, and later in the story bodily discomfort, and is represented by the prodigal son. The second part, as represented by the elder son, is, on the surface, the dutiful, responsible part, but mentally ruled by resentment, and seething with critical thoughts on unfairness and self-worth. The third part welcomes both 'body' and 'mind' into the celebration with the 'spirit'. Here we have a variation of sacred psychology comprising body (impulsive and selfish desires), mind (the ego or persona we present to the world) and spirit (a non-critical, accepting superego that can synthesise the other parts). Separated from each other, through denial or projection, each part experiences suffering – physically, mentally and spiritually. Integration and self-acceptance leaves us free to be truly alive and in the present. It leaves us free to be in an authentic relationship with God.

Kirsty

In the last chapter we left Kirsty experimenting with her imagination and creativity. She spoke about finding herself through these artistic activities. '*It* must have been there all along, but it is only now that I want and feel able to paint and mould the clay.' What was the '*it*' that she spoke about? It was an inner urge to create a painting, or to transform the clay into colourful and meaningful shapes. This ability emerged towards the end of Kirsty's therapy, and had true value. Other emotional experiences had emerged during the therapy, especially Kirsty's unhappiness and her anger. Earlier her unhappiness had been clouded by shame and guilt, and her anger by self-destructive behaviour. The clear feelings of unhappiness and anger also had true value, as distinct from their earlier deceptive appearances masked by drink and self-hatred. Such authentic psychic reality is not discernible, or something we learn about in an objective way; rather, we become it – or it becomes us. The process of therapy was for Kirsty a process for facilitating the emergence of what had true value. Her unhappiness and anger had been transformed into the energy to create.

Kirsty was grateful for discovering this aspect within her, and in her gratitude wanted to give something back. An opportunity arose when she saw a notice asking for volunteers at the local women's aid refuge. Kirsty offered to run an art group for some of the children staying at the refuge, and, together with the play worker, set up a weekly session in the house. This proved to be the start of a long involvement with the refuge, which eventually culminated in paid work. Kirsty explained that spending time with the children, who, like her, were also witnesses to domestic violence, helped her understand even more about her experiences. In her work with the children, she could also see their creative potential. It was as if through colour and shape a different perspective on the world could be experienced.

Kirsty's capacity to believe in something different, and the potential for change were established, but she had huge difficulties in relating to the idea of God at all, and especially to that of God the father. Despite the work we had done together on her relationship with her own aggressive and inconsistent father, Kirsty felt uncomfortable with this image of God. She found it difficult to move from the idea of God as a controlling and demanding parent, to one who might respect and encourage creativity and personal responsibility. The work with the children in the refuge also reinforced the experience of fathers as violent and frightening figures. The idea of God as mother was also unsatisfactory, as Kirsty associated this with her frightened, cowed mother who could not leave her husband, and sacrificed herself throughout Kirsty's childhood in a way that had engendered guilt in Kirsty as a child, and that the adult Kirsty now found unappealing.

Several years after we had finished our work together, Kirsty wrote to tell me about what had been happening to her, including a strange encounter on a train. Here's part of her letter.

> I was coming back from spending a few days with my daughter – she's working now in a hospital and really enjoying her work. She's also got a boyfriend, and amazingly he seems ok, not at all like her dad! Anyway, the train stopped (as they do) and went on stopping, and then we were told there was something wrong with the engine and we'd all have to get off at the next station and wait for it to be sorted. Everyone had begun talking in the carriage about what was wrong with the train, we were all being really friendly, and saying how we needed to get back or catch connections, and how awful the trains were.
>
> This really friendly – quite young (well younger than me!) man had been sitting opposite me, and as we waited at the station he told me he was due to lead a group and was going to be late. I asked him about it, and he told me he was a Franciscan monk – though he wasn't dressed in any special way – and so we got talking about religion and God. It was so strange, as I found myself saying some of the things we had talked about, and it seemed even clearer about my dad and my mum, and how the word 'father' made it hard to think about love and gentleness and so on.
>
> We went on talking – or rather I think I did most of it – it all seemed to pour out again, but he seemed interested, and not at all critical or off-putting. Just as we got to where I was getting off, he looked in his bag, and said

with a big smile – 'I've got just the book for you – would you like to read it?' He gave me this book – and said that inside was the address of his monastery, and when I'd finished I could send it back and tell him what I thought of it. I just felt so chuffed by the talking and his gift – I felt really *really* pleased and odd, as if I'd been given a big hug.

Kirsty went on to write that she'd read the book, and found it made so much sense. It was a book called *Memories of God* and was about the very things that had puzzled her for so long. In the end she'd bought her own copy of the book, and written back to the monk, and then he'd written back to her, and slowly Kirsty was beginning to see that these experiences of the past and the present could all be separated out. She added 'but I had to know it for myself, it had to be me feeling it, and not just being told – I really think that monk was brilliant – he turned up out of the blue – and with that book – very strange . . . now I'm just going to see what happens next – anything is possible!'

In the book that Kirsty read, Roberta Bondi describes what it meant for her to grow up female in terms of religious belief, and the effect of her own father on her relationship with God. 'As for God, I found that in public prayer, the very use of the name Father would regularly fill me with a sense of inadequacy, helplessness, and depression . . . For so many of us the language of God the Father, and our own painful experiences of ourselves and our human fathers, are tangled together.'[12]

Roberta Bondi writes how she found her way out of this tangle through the writings of the early monastic teachers.

> Unknown to me as the monks were, however, the contents of that book began to open my eyes at once to another reality, in which I would learn that God was very different from the one I had thought God to be, and that this was going to have immense repercussions for me.

What I read that day was an exhortation to those early monks not to criticise or judge each other, but rather, to treat each other with the gentleness of our heavenly father, who especially loves the ones the world despises, and who is always so much more willing than human beings to make allowances for sin, because God alone understands our circumstances, the depths of our temptations and the extent of our suffering ... I knew that somehow these people who lived nearly a millennium and a half ago had spoken to me directly out of their own love, and of God's love for me.

Roberta Bondi also picks up the difficulties around relating to God as children, and her assumption that we are being told to relate to that father 'as *very little* children relate to the kind of benevolent, dominant, parent who prefers toddlers to adolescents because toddlers are so sweet and adolescents are so complicated'. She explores the meaning of the story of the raising of Lazarus, and the parts played by Mary and Martha as Jesus' adult friends, who are neither submissive nor subservient; because they love him, they are not afraid of him and tell him they are angry and why. She points out that Jesus does not just put up with these women, he chooses and trusts them as his closest friends. She suggests that if we can accept the invitation to stand as adult friends of God we can set aside our damaged images of God's fatherhood and let our human fathers be our actual fathers, neither more nor less than who they really are.

The God of revelation

In the story of the prodigal son the father is revealed as a compassionate, loving and welcoming figure. He stands looking out for the lost son, and when he glimpses him still far away in the distance he runs to meet him – he does not just walk, he runs. In a similar way, God reached out to meet

Roberta Bondi through the writings of the early monastic teachers, and the love of God was revealed to Kirsty with her encounter with the stranger on the train. These are images of the God of revelation who comes willingly and eagerly to meet us in our yearning, our confusion and our distress. The God of revelation is the God who is experienced as present, and who calls for a response. He cannot be kept at arm's length and asks to be in relationship with us. He is not the silent or mute God of dogma and intellectual reason, but the God who speaks to people, sometimes through the Scriptures and other writings, sometimes through other people.

Thomas Merton explores the implications of God's revelation to Moses in Exodus 3. God has observed the sufferings of the Hebrews enslaved in Egypt. He says to Moses, 'I know their sufferings', and calls the reluctant Moses to lead the people to freedom. Realising that the people will want him to identify the God who is offering this deliverance to them, Moses asks the voice, 'When the people ask who is sending me, what name shall I give them?' The response YHWH is generally translated as 'I am who I am', and although interpreted in many ways, most of them suggest it is to do with the divine presence to the people.

> Yahweh is saying that he *will* be present, because He is the one who is present... Moses is aware of the altogether extraordinary and gratuitous reality of God's presence to him here at Horeb. This in itself constitutes and implies a promise of that same presence and powerful protection in the future. Thus the reality of Yahweh's presence... is... a *personal relationship* of a supremely religious kind... [Martin] Buber brings this out in his translation: 'I will be there as the *I* that will be there.'

For the Christian, the full significance of the Name that implies revelation, Thomas Merton believes, comes to light 'in

133

the Person of Jesus the living actual presence of the ineffable Name'.[13]

The message is that whoever we are, whatever we have done, and whatever has happened to us in the past, we are included in this invitation into relationship with God. God is there ready to reveal himself if we can have the capacity to turn from our self-absorption, and with trust and faith make this connection. We cannot control by our human will this experience of divine grace, but we can be open and aware enough to respond if and when it happens to us. In St Bernard's degrees of love we move in stage 3 ('We love God for himself') and stage 4 ('We love ourselves for God's sake') into grace-filled moments, when we are taken out of ourselves into another encounter.

Wisdom in relationship

Making such a connection with God can only develop if we are able to be in a wise relationship with our past, and fully alive in our present, and well able to tolerate being and thinking in the presence of another person. As has been explored in this book, this capacity to relate, badly affected by childhood difficulties, gradually needs to be re-established, and our ability to relate reaffirmed through actual experiences.

Martin Buber states that a person finds or discovers self in relationship – in dialogue with the other. It is through relationship that we grow, develop and mature, and it is the way through which the sense of our self gradually unfolds. 'In the beginning is the relation – as the category of being, as readiness, as a form that reaches out to be filled, as a model of the soul; the *a priori* of relation: *the innate You* . . . The development of the child's soul is connected indissolubly with his craving for the You . . . [This develops through] gradually entering into relationships . . . [We] becomes an I through a You.'[14]

As we rebuild our lives following a troubled childhood we

learn to relate again. This time our experiences include well-earned wisdom and insight.

Alan

In the last chapter we left Alan wondering what to do about his spiritual dilemmas. As a psychotherapist I could not answer his questions; although I felt they merited further enquiry, and I was very interested in them, I was not a spiritual teacher or working in that context. Answering such concerns requires, in my view, contact with someone who is part of a religious practice that has been developed specifically to help with such questions and issues. Alan was unsure how to proceed. He felt uncomfortable about going to church, and did not know whom to contact. He felt he did not want to be trapped in anything that might resemble his old family, where he would start to feel he had to be helpful or responsible – making coffee, giving lifts, and talking to people he did not want to be with. Although we had finished our work, I was curious about what happened to him, and very pleased when one evening, about a year after our last conversation, he rang to tell me.

Alan told me that initially he had let things drift. It had all felt too difficult and too much effort. Anyway, he was busy at work, and he and his girlfriend had made plans to get married, and were thinking about moving. There was a lot on, but it seemed as if the busier he was, the more he longed for time to spend in prayer or reading. He had found spiritual autobiographies especially helpful, but the library selection was pretty poor. Again he had found himself drawn to the large church in his town; there were often lots of tourists looking around, and Alan felt he could be anonymous there. One weekend, when his girlfriend was away, he had gone to a service of evening prayer. He had liked the fact he could just slip in there, watch what went on, and then leave, and thought he might try different services as well. The big surprise was that he found that both the team vicars were saying things in their sermons that he could understand and relate to. Neither seemed formal or stuffy and both were ordinary and approachable in a welcome low-key sort of way. One of the team vicars was a woman, and for both Alan and his girlfriend this turned out to be significant.

Alan's girlfriend now felt that if she wanted to, she could return to the church of her childhood. She had felt from her adolescence that it was an all-male club, and therefore one from which she felt rejected, and in which she was seen as inferior because she was female. For her the very presence of women priests in the church altered that feeling. Alan told me that for a start she felt the whole thing sounded better with both male and female voices. This led to their decision to get married in a church. Before that could happen, Alan realised that he also wanted to be able to take communion as part of his developing relationship with Jesus Christ, and so he began adult confirmation classes, led, by chance that year, by the woman vicar. This provided him with a forum to raise the very concerns that had been troubling him, but more importantly it gave him a context that nurtured and sustained him in his spiritual development.

The experience of regularly attending church and going to the weekly confirmation classes was important to him because it gave him a further chance to test out his new-found insights gained from analysis of his family relationships, including those with his mother. Although the confirmation class had met as a small group – there were only three of them that year taking the course – there was plenty of opportunity to explore individual concerns and talk through previously held assumptions about religion. Alan felt he had got really close to the others in the group.

Alan said it was different from therapy, as it seemed to be not about adjusting and accepting the past on his own, but rather about the present and the future in the light of Christ. He joked that another benefit was that what was being offered was free, and time and energy had been given so generously to the entire group. This I felt was also in part a sideways swipe at the therapy profession! For Alan, the experience was in the relationships he was making – both outside and within himself. He said that he felt really valued and accepted by both the vicars, and that the experience of sharing such serious thoughts in the group had left them all enriched and feeling very close to one another. At last here was a different sort of family experience led by a different sort of 'mother' from the one he had known as a child. This confirmed the type of relationship begun with me in the therapy. Gradually Alan was realising that he didn't have to feel responsible for keeping everything safe and well. He could see that the vicar was healthy, assured and mentally robust, and embodied the love of Christ that she was talking about.

Finally, Alan said, most importantly, that taking communion was like walking in a new world – both a celebration and intimate nurturing at the same time. Here was the ultimate in both 'mothering' and 'fathering'. He said that the Alan he offered to God was nothing to do with the false self Alan constructed on self-sacrifice and compliance, but instead something to do with his own fulfilment, and the realisation of his true self. Instead of a relationship held together by 'oughts' and 'shoulds', and fuelled by guilt, fear and anger, there was a wiser relationship with a foundation of love and acceptance, and fuelled by genuine desire and pure longing.

Thinking about this conversation reminded me of the importance that Thomas Merton placed on his own experience of the Eucharist. For him it was not just part of the formal act of worship, or a ritual commemoration of something that happened in the past, but a 're-presentation' of the mystery and events of redemption. He suggests that by taking Holy Communion we become united to Christ and through Christ to the Father through the Spirit of love. As we become united to Christ through the body and blood – the bread and the wine – we are also discovering our deepest identity. In the words of Thomas Merton, 'By our union with Christ in the Eucharist we find our true selves.'[15]

The final chapter looks more closely at this personal encounter with God through Jesus Christ, and adds some concluding thoughts to spiritual recovery from a troubled childhood. We move away from the format of exploring a particular story and route on our journeying home. Clearly we all have different psychic constitutions and different life experiences but, as the stories of Kirsty and Alan have shown, we all have the capacity to be open to a spiritual life. We leave Kirsty and Alan taking new directions and no longer limited and so stuck in the past. We also move on from the story of the prodigal son that has been central to our inner journeying of body, mind and spirit. The son was able to take a hard look at his situation and where his responses and behaviour had brought him. As he thought and acknowledged what had happened to him, and what had led to his state of despair, he was able to make a move, leave his exile and return home.

CHAPTER EIGHT

Held in love-scarred hands

Life has seasons
so weary, worn and sad
that the only hand to reach for
is one love-scarred,
the only comfort
to recline on the bosom
of Him Who knew none,
to drink from his cup,
to welcome
His wounding touch
And being so smitten
(O Lord, I am not worthy)
healed.[1]

JOURNEYING HOME STARTS with a glimpse of recognition that something needs to change. We are interrupted by a thought: 'Is this it?' 'Is this how it's always going to be?' 'I don't want to spend my life like this!' 'There has to be something more!' We wake up to the realisation that something needs to happen. Journeying home is an awakening, a way of happening, and a relationship – with ourselves and then with God.

If we can move to compassion and love ourselves for ourselves, and away from a distorted self-love or even self-hatred, then we can move to love God for what he gives us. Understanding our past, and our hang-ups and difficulties in relationship, can free us to better accept God and his love for us. Sometimes therapy and counselling can help us reach the first degree of love in St Bernard's description, and help us to appreciate the second, but it is then that therapy is left behind and we move into the spiritual inner journey of stages three and four. This is something for us to come back to in the final part of this chapter.

On the routes taken on our journeying home therapy and religion have jostled side by side, sometimes overlapping and sometimes veering apart. We need now to understand the relationship between them and look and see what the difference is between being 'in therapy' and leading a spiritual life.

The history of suspicion between religion and psychotherapy probably began with Freud's Enlightenment message that religion was only a vestige of infantile needs and guilt. This did not endear him to the religious establishment. Jung, who incorporated religious symbols into the somewhat introverted task of individuation, suggested that each of us carries the collective wisdom of the human race within the self – perhaps with the implication that each person could be his or her own church. Again not a message totally welcomed by any religious institution. In contemporary times dialogue has become increasingly possible through the development of interpersonal theory, object relations theory and social psychology. However, much psychological thinking seems to assume that religious experiences and religious relationships can only be understood in the context of our own mental activity. There is little acceptance of any real relationship between humans and a divine Being who is both immanent and transcends human perception and language. It is hardly surprising then that the church sometimes views psychotherapy with concern.

In the biblical stories explored we have considered therapeutic and religious ideas that seem to be the same, but now if we look more closely we can see that the religious ideas have a deeper meaning and different implications. One of these is linked to the idea of 'holding', another to the 'true' and 'false' self concepts, and a third to the idea of change and transformation.

Feeling held

'We must give up trying to hold His hand, and just stretch out our hands – even if they are just fists – for God to hold. There is all the difference ... between holding and being held.'[2]

What does it mean to feel held? Most of us have a sense of security when this is happening although, again, this is one of those ambiguous words – like forgiveness and love – that describes an experience, a sensation and a state of mind. Donald Winnicott, the analyst and paediatrician quoted in earlier parts of this book, wrote about the importance of the 'holding environment' leading to the belief in the reliability of inner processes, and the establishment of the sense of oneself. If our earliest environment, made up of our parent(s) and the way mother or the mothering person treats us, is 'good enough', to use another of Donald Winnicott's phrases, then we thrive. In this phase that belongs in infancy, the small baby moves from a stage of absolute dependency to relative dependency as a toddler, and then towards independence as a small child. If the infant's needs are met in a loving and reliable way that is both physically and emotionally 'good-enough', the growing child feels they are 'held'.[3] We can see it in secure children, who carry a certain inner sureness and confidence.

When Donald Winnicott was sixty-seven he wrote a poem

called 'The Tree' (before going to boarding school he would do his homework in a special tree in the garden), which includes the following lines:

> Mother below is weeping
> > weeping
> > weeping
> Thus I knew her
>
> Once, stretched out on her lap
> > as now on dead tree
> I learned to make her smile
> > to stem her tears
> > to undo her guilt
> > to cure her inward death
> To enliven her was my living

As Adam Phillips explains, in the poem Donald Winnicott clearly identifies himself with Christ and the tree of the title is the cross. Adam Phillips suggests that the poem recalls an early experience of Donald Winnicott's mother's depression, and her consequent inability to emotionally hold him.

The poem speaks of the absence of what became, in Winnicott's developmental theory, the formative experience in the child's life: the way the mother, in the fullest sense, 'holds' the child, which includes the way the child is held in the mother's mind as well as in her arms. The infant's first environment, in Winnicott's terms, is the experience of being held.[4]

It seems that he felt, as some children do, that his sacrifice was metaphorically to die to enable his mother to live. Children who grow up with this anxiety become very good at anticipating the responses and reading the reactions of those they are with – and so often become therapists!

As 'the talking cure', analytic work involves language. This can become a metaphor for our experiences when we were very young, so we speak of holding and containing, feeding and nurturing, and murderous rage and destruction, yet the experience feels at times tangible. For example, we might feel *as if* we could go and murder someone, but by talking about it we don't have to! Good therapeutic work gives the person coming for therapy the experience of being held – we *can* be held by another's knowledge and understanding of our deepest fears and feelings, but through words and not physically. We can describe it as 'being held in mind' – and appreciate a feeling of being thought about in a helpful way. Over time this experience becomes internalised and part of our inner world. There is, then, the blueprint for acknowledging that we are held by God, based on our known experience of faith, trust and belief.

'Loving God, from birth to death, you hold us in your hand.'[5] In the quotation by George Hodgkin, at the start of this section, he speaks of being held by God. This religious understanding is different from the analytic perspective as it is a reversal of our development as small children. With God we move from independence where we feel in charge (or not) of our lives, through to relative dependency – where we hold on to God when we remember to, or need to – to a final realisation and a place of absolute surrender, not as a helpless and tiny baby, but in the sense that our life is in Christ and that we are held in that faith. It is grace and an experience of something done to us as distinct from our attempts to make it happen. Paul Tillich uses the expression 'struck by grace' to describe the moment of awareness that captures the justifying moment, the moment that tells us we are accepted, and held by God, in spite of everything we know against ourselves.[6]

One of the suggestions in this book has been that sometimes, because of what happened in the past, we cannot fully allow ourselves this experience of being held by God and dependent on him. Repairing the damage takes place as we gradually uncover, through the stories of healing, our states of stuckness, and allow our feelings to be expressed, and our thinking to become less restricted. If we can develop from a place of distorted dependency we free ourselves to enter willingly into a relationship of healthy, mature dependency with the Being who knows us better than we can ever know ourselves. It's as if the dark cloud at the edge of our life, spoken about in Chapter 1, has finally drifted right away, and our horizons have clearly opened up.

The move from false to true self in therapy and in spiritual life

One of the ideas thought about in our journeying home is the move from false self to true self. We have looked at the analytic (Donald Winnicott) and religious (Thomas Merton) ways that these terms are used. So is there then any real difference between them? I think the religious meaning of true self encompasses something far deeper than our individuality, but we need to explore this further.

Both Thomas Merton and Donald Winnicott write about our false self as masking our true self, so the false self is not what or who we are. Donald Winnicott also thought that sometimes the false self works to protect and care-take the true self until it is able to emerge. As we journey through our past and acknowledge the way that early experiences have affected us, and our relations with others, we start to rid ourselves of our false self and deepen our self-awareness.

Ultimately, though therapy is our journey out into the world, it is a self-seeking process of building up rather than stripping down. We can be repaired in our sense of who we are and what we can accomplish; our sense of being nothing and easily overwhelmed can be replaced by feeling we are someone who can cope. If we go for therapy, or do our own self-analysis, we are usually aiming to feel more at home – better integrated – if not successful in the world. We are aiming to 'love ourselves for ourselves'. We may also develop to a place where we 'love our therapist for what he or she has given us'! The implicit message of most therapy is that we are worthy of love for our own sake. In our true self we realise our potential as an individual.

Thomas Merton writes that 'The person must be rescued from the individual.' He urges each of us as the 'free child of God'[7] to recognise that we are found and loved by God, and without him and his mercy we have nothing and need everything. Thomas Kelly describes it as 'an increased awareness of a more-than-ourselves, working persuadingly and powerfully at the roots of our own soul, and in the depths of all'.[8] A mature and serious Christian life is an integration of our true self in the encounter with Christ. In this sense we have recognised that we are someone, but can experience our own nothingness and insufficiency. In this relationship Christ becomes the 'more-than-ourselves' centre through whom and by whom we live, and in whom we see our place in the world. Christ not only guides and teaches us what the Christian life should be, but restores that life to us through the action of the Spirit. Somewhere in our journeying there is a turning within to meet a part of ourselves which has never been away from our real home, and that welcomes us back to unity in the central and truest part of our existence.

Death to resurrection – change and transformation

Most of us, whatever our childhood experiences, are consciously or unconsciously looking for a confessor or a witness – someone with whom to share our story. Much therapy takes place in the Saturday before the resurrection in the darkness of despair and pain. In the place of darkness there is always a kernel of hope that change might be possible. Indeed the assertion of hope is present as we take the first step on the journey to change how we feel. It is at that point that we have made a decision to move from being a victim to someone who makes a choice. The choice we can make is about how we respond to what we feel, how we choose to behave in relationship with others, and the way we lead our life. Understanding cannot change the past but it can change the way we respond. Julian of Norwich knew a lot about past pain and brokenness and said, 'Although a soul's wounds heal, the scars remain; God sees them not as blemishes but as honours.'[9] When we move from victim to 'chooser',[10] then transformation and change has begun.

This is the case whether we try to analyse ourselves, or whether we seek out help from someone else. The main thing is for us to listen to our own story, and if possible be listened to. This is the start of the change and transformation. Psychoanalytic and psychodynamic technique is merely technique and in that sense is morally neutral. It is neither good nor bad in itself; it is rather a way of uncovering what lies beneath our surface thinking. All depends on the person who is using it, and the spirit in which it is being used, as this affects the quality of the therapeutic relationship.

The change and transformation sought through therapy is different from that found through spiritual life, although there is some overlap. Both are about a form of relational knowledge. We change ourselves through the relationship with the therapist, and we are changed in our relationship with God. When we feel better we move on and leave the therapist, although the relationship remains in our mind, but ideally our relationship with God deepens and intensifies. Psychological health is about adjusting our behaviour, emotional state and thinking to the way of the world and to each other. Our mental condition is improved through psychic change. Spiritual health is about becoming rather than adjusting. In spiritual health we experience God as our centre: 'In Him we live and move and have our being' (Acts 17:28). Our souls are saved through spiritual change.

A final change and transformation in spiritual life is that we become part of a worldwide community of other believers – we are no longer alone and we try to love one another. Then we can recognise how the true encounter with Christ 'liberates something in us, a power we did not know we had, a hope, a capacity for life, a resilience, an ability to bounce back when we thought we were completely defeated, a capacity to grow and change, a power of creative transform-ation'.[11] The living Christ has overcome anything that might seem to block both our human and spiritual growth.

'Give sorrow words'[12]

On this journey we have read about different stories – sorrow has been put into words. The journeying has been set within three great biblical narratives, and the examples used have been narratives from literature and from the personal stories brought by Kirsty and Alan, which are an amalgam of my own personal and professional experience. We all try to make sense of our lives by organising and turning key events into stories that then become part of our larger life narrative. Our stories about ourselves help us to live, and the words that we use conjure up worlds for ourselves and for others. In a sense our stories hold us together – and also distinguish us from each other.

As we explored at the start of the book, a troubled child-hood ruptures our sense of well-being, and disrupts our storyline about ourselves and how we make sense of our relationships. We are left feeling that we have been formed by uncontrollable factors. This journey has been in part about the process of putting all that into words. Body sensations, raw emotions, vulnerable feelings can all be expressed and contained through words, and this helps us manage and cope with our experiences. There is a tremendous relief in har-nessing what previously felt fragmented into phrases and expression, and a story that we can repeat and draw on to explain and gain insight, rather than something to be denied or avoided at all costs.

The three biblical narratives used as a framework: Peter's betrayal of Jesus and his story of guilt and forgiveness, the slavery in Egypt and the exodus to the Promised Land, and the account of the exile in Babylon and the return home, have been reinterpreted and adapted to help in the journey to spiritual recovery. All three stress that each stuck state has its counterpart and route out. Each story reflects a particular focus: on the body, mind or spirit, although they are clearly interconnected. Each of the three stories used, and the story of the prodigal son that was included in each chapter, is also a revelation of God and God's presence beside us as we journey.

As we stumble about in our own darkness we are not alone. The Christ of the 'love-scarred hands' is ever present driving us to a light that can truly free us from past pain. This is the Jesus described in the gospels who in his ministry and in the manner of his death identified with, and strengthened, the powerless, the damaged and the imprisoned. Rowan Williams writes, 'God becomes recognisable as God only at the place of extremity, where no answers seem to be given and God cannot be seen as the God we expect or understand.'[13] The task is to let go of our own expectations and understanding, and take a leap of faith. The resurrection that happened to Jesus is also something that we are called to experience in our own lives. This is the dynamic of transformation – the dynamic that emerges in our relationship with God that allows us to accept ourselves and move on.

Some suggestions

This book has made four main suggestions, which inevitably overlap with one another. The first and central idea has been about the need to confront and integrate difficulties from the past in order to open up our relationship with God. The three biblical stories and the journeys made by others suggest how we can know ourselves in all our pain, upset and anger. We can see how the past has affected us physically (in psycho-somatic symptoms and through our sense of our body), mentally (in the way we have restricted our thinking or not thought at all), and spiritually (in our lack of imagination and inhibited capacity to believe). With this recognition come understanding, insight and compassion. The past is never changed, but the way we choose to respond to what has happened to us can be significantly altered.

The second suggestion is closely related and links to the notion of spiritual pathology. We need to disentangle genuine motives from our own self-deception. Again as the stories have shown us, it is surprisingly easy to distort and contaminate our spiritual relationship and awareness because of our own individual psychopathology. Perhaps we sometimes fit our image of God to familiar patterns based on other sometimes damaging relationships. As this way of thinking is so embedded within us, we do not see what we are doing, and cannot understand why our spiritual life seems unsatisfactory and so predictable. As Alan showed us, it is relatively easy to turn our own needs into a religion – almost to the extent of worshipping our personal weaknesses. Accompanying this is the delusion around our self-beliefs that we are completely right in what we are doing or believing. In that way our religious practices can be a rationalisation, or even a justification, for our personal hang-ups. Unfortunately there are very few places where this can be openly discussed and understood. Inevitably what is personal can also be collective, and we can be attracted to groups or institutions that unconsciously collude with our pathology. Organisational pathology sadly is not uncommon, leading us far from the example of Jesus Christ.

The third suggestion we've looked at in the book is that a therapeutic relationship, either in a pastoral setting, or outside the religious context, can help to kick-start our spiritual life. We can move from being spiritually dead to a rebirth or nativity of the soul. If we are listened to and understood, if we are thought about and reliably held in mind by someone new, our inner foundations of trust, belief and faith are built up. We need this experience so that we can turn in maturity to an authentic relationship with God. Of course, we do not know how the Spirit moves and do not always realise through what experiences and relationships we receive God's grace. In a sense all is interconnected, in that we need faith to recognise God's grace, and vice versa, that we need God's grace to accept faith. If we are locked in pain and hatred we cannot love and we cannot forgive, and something or somebody needs to help us interrupt this captivity.

The fourth main suggestion is about sacred psychotherapy or pastoral psychotherapy, in other words, that religion and psychology can both enrich one another and that it is possible for the two to work together despite their differences. This book reflects a need of our own day that looks for a rapprochement between therapy and spirituality as 'theology bred in the crucible of experience',[14] and our involvement with a healing God who is with us, whether we know it or not, through times of trouble and pain.

Perhaps the place where therapy and spirituality most overlap lies in contemplative prayer. The contemplative tradition in Christianity is more than just an exercise in prayer, in that it inevitably involves both the seeking of God and the coming to know one's true self, as well as learning one's relationship to the world. Contemplation calls for acquaintance with our inner world, and all our weaknesses and faults. Much contemplative prayer initially may take the form of seeing the nature of distracting thoughts, and grieving for the past. In this way such meditation in the presence of God has the quality of free association in the analytic tradition – letting thoughts come to mind without repressing them. It becomes a space where the usual constraints of time and space do not apply, and the difference between what is inside us and outside us is less distinct. Some people feel that such self-examination or preoccupation is indulgent or morbid and does not belong in a life of prayer, but as we can see it is better to own and explore feelings, both good and bad, than banish them as unsuitable or unwholesome in some way.

Contemplation might also take the form of telling the story of parts of our life – the painful times and some of the good parts as well – in the presence of God. Perhaps we can also distinguish old familiar images and attributes that we have projected onto God, and some that have been given to us as well: including the familiar god who compares, rewards and punishes us; the white, male misogynist patriarch; and the god out there and above us who searches out every sin with a terrible look. As Paul Tournier writes: 'In our spiritual lives there are plenty of events, impulses, and inspirations that we attribute to God, when in fact they are the outcome of unconscious urges. Religious meditation, as well as technical analysis, can help us to recognise this. There are also real interventions by the Spirit.'[15]

Paul Tournier acknowledges that from the perspective of psychological phenomena it is all only a matter of mental functions. But from the perspective of faith it is possible to see behind the interplay of these functions to the great struggle going on between the Spirit and the parts of us that resist our sincerest attempts to obey God. This he refers to as the drama of our spiritual destiny. He adds that in this way the honesty that is fostered by our psychological analysis continually refines our spiritual life.

Our spiritual knowledge is situated in our experience and embodied within us. It is different for each of us. Although what is absolute and what is relative are both present, our minds are limited in their capacity to grasp this. In meeting God we need to try to let go of our definitions, and our psychotherapeutic and religious perspectives and insights, and trust the relationship with him as best we can. If we allow it this will be an experience that is 'Other', and unlike any other relationship we have known. Ultimately we need, when we are able to do this, to meet him in silence and in the present moment and to let God's silence work on us. We have then finally returned home. As Merton expresses it, 'In contemplation, as we let go of words and concepts as a way of relating to God, we enter God's silence in the depth of our being.'[16]

St Bernard's four stages in the journey to love

We love ourselves for ourselves.
We love God for what he gives us.
We love God for Himself.
We love ourselves for God's sake.

In St Bernard's four stages we see a journey of change from self-centredness to God-centredness. It is a risking all – a falling in love with God and finding everything and everybody in him. St Bernard tells us that it is only as we come to love God for himself, willing to lose all, that we can come to love everything in him including loving ourselves for God's sake.[17] This is losing life to find it. In these stages we will find the ground of our being – our own inmost spiritual depths – with God who is always present in these same depths. When we know God, we will truly know ourselves, and the two will merge at the final point.

The language of psychotherapy concentrates on the individual self, with words about personal integration and self-fulfilment. The language of spirituality and religion speaks about a letting go and dying to self. However, in the end language about God gives way to silence, as St Bernard's journey moves us into a deeper and different level of reality, a level of mystery and the unknown. This is the place of the spiritual unconscious beyond and above the individual unconscious 'with its superficial enjoyments and fears'.[18] This is not an unconsciousness to be rationally brought to our reasoned consciousness but an Otherconscious realm of pure mystery. Here there are no maps or clear paths for the journey: the route is surrender.

Geography comes to an end,
Compass has lost all earthly north,
Horizons have no meaning
Nor roads an explanation.[19]

FURTHER IDEAS, EXERCISES AND PRAYERS

➤⬅

THESE ARE WAYS of helping to think about unresolved painful events from childhood. They cannot replace the experience of talking to someone about the past, but they can help provide a framework to using the book.

Allowing memories and reflections about the past to come to mind

Memories can arise at any time, and sometimes in a way that we do not want. Perhaps when you try to clear your mind to meditate or pray there are confusing thoughts or distressing feelings. A quiet time can be set aside to think about what these are. It is useful to have a framework so that your thinking can be managed and contained (as much as is possible) to within a certain time limit (e.g. 15 minutes). It can help to write down in a journal what you feel.

Relaxing and centring

Find a comfortable place and position. Try to relax by stretching and relaxing each part of the body in turn, beginning with the soles of the feet and slowly moving upwards to the top of the head. This should leave you relaxed in body and yet alert in mind.

A simple breathing exercise can help your breathing to slow and deepen. Gently begin to breathe from the diaphragm instead of from the top of the chest, and with the deepening slow the breath. Try to breathe like this for a few minutes before settling to a level that feels more comfortable. The aim is to be relaxed. If feelings arise try to breathe out the negative states of mind, and breathe in the positive and affirming. For example breathe out shame and guilt, and breathe in acceptance and forgiveness.

Ask God for his help and guidance in spiritual recovery from the past.

> *Dear God, I need your help in doing this. Be with me so I can be strong and manage to cope. Hold me in your loving hands and protect me from all danger.*

Working on feelings

Not everyone feels comfortable talking about feelings. One way to help if you are stuck is to make a list of all sorts of feelings, then add to it by listing the opposite feelings. Recall events in your life, then add different feelings to each event. Another way is to note down feelings in the journal, especially when the feelings are strong and negative.

Getting in touch with rage and anger is an important step in recovery. The first step is to recognise that anger and allow it. Who are you angry with? Who are you most angry with? Your parents? God? The world? Yourself? How do you usually manage rage? For example do you keep quiet? Or do you break things?

It can sometimes be helpful to write a letter to the person or people who have hurt you (even if the person is no longer alive). This is a letter that expresses all your rage, but it is not a letter that is sent. The letter can be kept and added to, or it can be ripped up or burnt. Being angry with someone and expressing it helps you feel whole again. It does not preclude remembering the good things about that person as well.

Sometimes it helps to follow the same sort of exercise with fear: identify what you are frightened about and think through how this could be eased.

It's useful to have a list of good things that help you feel better. Often physical exercise helps, or listening to music, or holding on to something special such as a stone or a soft toy, or writing a message with your strengths (see the shield idea below) or some Bible passages that you find especially helpful to read.

Writing a journal

The journal can be used when you are consciously remembering the past, or to jot down thoughts as they arise. It's also useful to keep it beside the bed to record dreams. Perhaps include photographs, or try drawing what you are remembering if it seems easier. It is helpful to date entries. This can be important when looking back and seeing connections and the pattern of God's movement in your life. The secret is to be completely honest. Perhaps, with something particularly painful, write it down in the form of a letter to God.

Reading back over the journal at regular intervals gives a chance to reflect on how much things have changed. Alternatively if it all seems rather stuck, perhaps share this with someone who can guide you through this.

How to start writing a journal

What has been happening over the last twenty-four hours? Who have you met, what have you done, what have you been thinking about? Can you write down your feelings about the day? Try not to hold anything back.

Imagine a twenty-four-hour clock. What time is it on the clock at this time of your life, and why? Write about this. Is it too late for . . .? Is it too soon for . . .? Now is the time for . . .

Begin to think about your childhood. Try drawing a shield divided into four quarters. Each quarter represents a section of childhood – say 0–5 years, 5–10 years, 10–15 years and 15–20 years. Alternatively, divide the shield in a way that better suits your experiences. In each section try to remember one good experience or one good relationship that happened during that time. This is something to which you can return and hold on to, if more negative experiences emerge.

Try to remember that if painful and angry feelings emerge from the past, you are experiencing what you may not have been able to feel at the time. In your journal try to write the feelings down, but add that 'this is what I felt when I was small.' Remind yourself that as an adult you have words and other resources to be able to manage the feelings.

Interpreting your dreams

Dreams can be complicated with no immediate sense to them, or really quite simple to understand. Most dreams, even the most apparently inconsequential, reveal something about the internal world. Try to remember a dream and write it down; think about your associations to what happened in the dream. Does the setting remind you of somewhere and what are your associations to that place? Who was in the dream, and are these important or unknown figures? The dream is your dream, so in that sense all those in the dream are figures in your internal world, and different parts or representing different attributes within your own self. Does the dream link back to events from the previous day? Can you access any feelings that were present in the dream, or later when you remembered it? All such thinking opens up your internal world and allows reflection on what we may prefer not to think about.

Linking to different chapters
Chapters 2 and 3

In her book *Open to God* (London: Hodder & Stoughton, 1989) Joyce Huggett offers some helpful ideas on forgiveness, which I have adapted to include here.

Begin to remember a time that feels particularly raw and painful. If it feels possible watch an action replay of the situation, though you can always switch the replay off at any time. Recall the person or people who were mainly involved. Then bring Jesus into the picture and introduce him to the people that you are remembering. If possible express to the individuals and to Jesus the hurt, the anger and the confusion you still feel about what happened. Speak about your resentments. Then watch and listen as Jesus interacts with these people who have hurt you. Do not force yourself to forgive if that does not yet feel right, but do keep at the back of your minds the phrase 'forgive . . . as we forgive'. Ask yourself whether you can accept that the feelings belong in the past, and so let go of them.

If you can let go of the feelings and start to forgive the person and yourself, the following rituals may be helpful.

First of all, return to relaxing and centring. Then breathe deeply and as you do breathe in the healing love of Jesus. As you breathe out let go of all the poisonous feelings you have been holding.

With the second ritual, find a stone or a piece of wood from outside that seems to embody your feelings of anger and grief. Holding it tightly, take this to a special place where you can sit to reflect. Slowly place the object in that space. If you feel able, pray the prayer Jesus prayed from the cross: 'Father, forgive them, for they do not know what they are doing.' Cup your empty hands as a sign that you are ready to receive God's love for the person who has abused and bruised your soul, and his healing for the wounds to your psyche.

If you cannot let go of the feelings and forgive those involved, tell Jesus what you are feeling. Imagine that your rage and hatred is embodied in a figure, which you then introduce to Jesus. Watch, as Jesus both accepts this part of you and wants to help you change it.

*Loving God, who accepts me for who I am, no matter
how awful I feel, help me to know and believe that
you love and forgive me.*

*Dear God, hold me close to you and have compassion
for me in my distress. Help me to let go of the past
and forgive those involved.*

Chapters 4 and 5

Try the exercise that Kirsty does in Chapter 5, by drawing a
tree of life. Start from your earliest roots and branches, noting
down events that happened and the fruits that you feel
resulted from these experiences. Are the fruits mainly mixed
– positive and negative? If they are predominantly one or the
other you may be denying your true feelings.

Try to write about how you now see yourself as you were
as a small child – as a ten-year-old – as a teenager. Can you
get in touch with any specific incidents or feelings linked to
those times? Describe what you remember and see if you can
recall what you felt at that particular age. Is there any particular incident that stands out? As an adult can you make
better sense of it all?

*Dear God, please, free me from my fear and anxieties;
help me to think differently and through your love
and grace, to become closer to you.*

*Jesus Christ, you understand what it feels like to be
a captive. Help me to know that I am not alone.
Release all of us who are lost and alone.*

Chapters 6 and 7

If our imagination and creativity is in exile, then we need to
try to open up this part of ourselves. One exercise I found
helpful was when I was given a book of modern art to look
at for a couple of days. I'm not artistic but the person helping

me suggested I just look through the book, not reading any-thing about the pictures, but gradually selecting my favourites. I found myself taking a long time with each picture, coming back to the book after a walk or a meal and looking again at the colour or detail. I was surprised with the favourite pictures that I chose.

Another route is through music or poetry, or dance. It doesn't matter what it is, there is no right or wrong – what matters is the process of releasing our imagination and our own creative ability. If we can become absorbed in the present moment then we move out of our place of exile. We can practise bringing ourselves back to the present moment – the feel of the sun or wind or rain, the light, our sense of our surroundings, how we are at that moment, what we are seeing or hearing or tasting.

Jesus Christ, help me to leave the place of exile and return home. Guide me and show me the way to my true self.

Dear Creator God, help me to love this life and the beauty of your world. Help me to come home to the best of who I am, and to influence others who are lost.

NOTES AND REFERENCES

Frontispiece quotation is from Rowan Williams, *Christ on Trial* (London: Fount, 2000), p. 138.

Introduction
1. St Bernard of Clairvaux, *On the Love of God*, trans. a Religious of CSMV (London and Oxford: A. R. Mowbray, 1950), and quoted in Brother Bernard, *Open to God* (London: Fount Paperbacks, 1986), p. 68.

Chapter One: Making sense of our past
1. Dylan Thomas, *Quite Early One Morning* (London and Melbourne: J. M. Dent & Sons Ltd, 1987).
2. The Charles Mitchener interview with V. S. Naipaul appeared in *Newsweek*, 16 November 1981, and is quoted by Lenore Terr MD in her book, *Too Scared to Cry, Psychic Trauma in Childhood* (New York: Harper & Row, 1990), p. 36. The quotations are from *The Enigma of Arrival* (London: Penguin, 1989), pp. 52 and 140.
3. George Orwell, 'Such, such were the joys' in *A Collection of Essays* (San Diego/New York: Harcourt Brace Jovanovich, 1947), pp. 1–47.
4. Leonard Shengold, 'The effects of child abuse as seen in adults', *Psychoanalytic Quarterly* 54 (1985), 20–45.
5. Howard Cooper, '"It is Torah and I have to learn": talking turkey about the body', *British Journal of Psychotherapy* 18/3 (2002), 349–60.
6. Marcus J. Borg, *Meeting Jesus Again for the First Time* (New York: HarperSanFrancisco, 1995).

Chapter Two: States of shame and guilt
1. Marcus J. Borg, *Meeting Jesus Again for the First Time* (New York: HarperSanFrancisco, 1995), p. 127. In a later footnote (p. 139 fn. 15) Borg stresses that by using the term 'priestly' he does not mean the 'priestly' or 'P' source of the Pentateuch.
2. Thomas Merton, *The Seven Storey Mountain* (New York: Signet Books, Harcourt, Brace & Co., Inc., 1948), extracts from pp. 13 and 14.

3. Fiona Gardner, 'Beyond gender', *The Merton Journal* (2002), Advent issue.
4. Thomas Merton, *The New Man* (New York: Farrar, Straus & Giroux, 1961), p. 73.
5. Maya Angelou, *Gather Together in My Name* (London: Virago, 1985), p. 6.
6. Henri J. M. Nouwen, *The Return of the Prodigal Son* (London: Darton, Longman & Todd, 1994), p. 36.
7. John Milton, *Paradise Lost* (London: Penguin, 1996), Book IV lines 108–10, p. 88.

Chapter Three: Movement to acceptance and forgiveness

1. Philip Roth, *The Human Stain* (London: Vintage, 2001), p. 314.
2. Una O'Higgins O'Malley, 'Forgiveness', *Spirituality* 8 (May/June 2002), 133.
3. C. G. Jung, *Psychology and Religion: West and East* (London and Henley: Routledge & Kegan Paul, 1977), p. 341. This includes the Faust quote.
4. David Bryant, 'Face to faith', *The Guardian*, 16 March 2002.
5. Walter Trobisch, *Love Yourself* (Downers Grove, Ill.: InterVarsity Press, 1976), pp. 231–2, quoted by Philip Yancey in *'What's So Amazing about Grace?'* (Grand Rapids, Mich.: Zondervan, 1997), p. 184.
6. Thomas Merton, *The Seven Storey Mountain* (New York: Harcourt, Brace & Co., 1948), extracts from pp. 354, 355 and 361.
7. Karl Barth, *The Word of God and the Word of Man* (New York: Harper & Row, 1957), p. 92, quoted in Yancey, *'What's So Amazing?'*, p. 271.
8. Henri J. M. Nouwen, *The Return of the Prodigal Son* (London: Darton, Longman & Todd, 1994), p. 130.
9. Mary Tighe, 'The challenge of letting God love us', *Spirituality* 8 (July/August 2002), 195.
10. Lewis B. Smedes, *Shame and Guilt* (San Francisco: HarperCollins, 1993), pp. 136, 141, quoted in Yancey, *'What's So Amazing?'*, p. 99.

Chapter Four: State of oppression

1. Marcus J. Borg, *Meeting Jesus Again for the First Time* (New York: HarperSanFrancisco, 1995), pp. 122–3.
2. Maurice Samuel (trans.), *Haggadah of Passover* (New York: Hebrew Publishing, 1942), quoted by Borg, *Meeting Jesus Again* (italics and language modified for gender-inclusive language), pp. 123 and 138.
3. Agneta Schreurs, *Psychotherapy and Spirituality* (London: Jessica Kingsley, 2002), p. 105.
4. Nick Hornby, *About a Boy* (London: Penguin, 2000), pp. 58 and 101.
5. Lenore Terr MD, *Too Scared to Cry* (New York: Harper & Row, 1990), p. 182.
6. Leonard Shengold, 'The effects of childhood abuse as seen in adults', *Psychoanalytic Quarterly* 54 (1990), p. 28; see also, for a discussion on

George Orwell's use of the idea of 'doublethink', Leonard Shengold, *Soul Murder Revisited* (New Haven and London: Yale University Press, 1999).

7. Shengold, 'Effects of childhood abuse', p. 29.

8. George Orwell, *1984* (London: Penguin, 1989), pp. 56, 62, 262 and 269.

9. Orwell, *1984*, p. 37.

10. Peter Fonagy, 'Thinking about thinking: some clinical and theoretical considerations in the treatment of a borderline patient', *International Journal of Psychoanalysis* 72/4 (1991), 639–56.

11. Sigmund Freud, 'Jensen's Gradiva' in James Strachey (ed.), *The Standard Edition of the Complete Psychological Works of Sigmund Freud* (London: Hogarth Press, 1907), Vol. IX, p. 35.

12. Richard Appignanesi and Zarate Oscar, *Freud for Beginners* (London: Writers and Readers Publishing Co-operative, 1979), p. 40.

13. Jolande Jacobi, *The Psychology of C. G. Jung* (London and Henley: Routledge & Kegan Paul, 1968), pp. 132–3.

14. Charles Odier, *Anxiety and Magic Thinking* (New York: International Universities Press, 1956), p. 135.

Chapter Five: Freedom to think

1. A saying from Poemen (200), in *Sayings of the Desert Fathers*, trans. Benedicta Ward (Oxford: Mowbray, 1981), p. 194, quoted by Roberta C. Bondi in 'Be not afraid: praying to God the Father', *Modern Theology* 9 (1993), 235–48.

2. Thomas Merton, *The New Man* (New York: Farrar, Straus & Giroux, 1961), p. 63.

3. Merton, *The New Man*, p. 67.

4. Peter Gay, *Freud* (London and Melbourne: J. M. Dent & Sons Ltd, 1988), p. 608.

5. An interesting summary of the central issues in *Moses and Monotheism* can be found in *The Oxford Companion to the Bible*, ed. Bruce M. Metzger and Michael D. Coogan (New York and Oxford: Oxford University Press, 1993), pp. 234 and 235.

6. This is a line taken from W. H. Auden's poem, 'In Memory of Sigmund Freud' in *W. H. Auden*, The Penguin Poets (Harmondsworth: Penguin, 1958), p. 68.

7. Sigmund Freud, quoted in The Institute of Psycho-Analysis, *Events* (Spring 1997).

8. Brian Keenan, *An Evil Cradling* (London: Vintage, 1992), p. 296.

9. Terry Waite, *Taken on Trust* (London: Hodder & Stoughton, 1993), pp. 454, 458 and 460.

10. Christopher Bollas, *Forces of Destiny* (London: Free Association Books, 1989), p. 197.

11. A useful introduction to the work of Wilfred Bion is found in Joan

and Neville Symington, *The Clinical Thinking of Wilfred Bion* (London and New York: Routledge, 1996); the quotation is taken from p. 84.

Chapter Six: State of estrangement

1. Trevor Dennis, 'Lament and complaint' in John Parr and Katharine Dell (eds), *Guidelines* 18/1 (Oxford: Bible Reading Fellowship, 2002), p. 60.
2. George Orwell, *1984* (London: Penguin, 1989), p. 62.
3. Andrew Mein, 'Ezekiel' in John Parr and Katharine Dell (eds), *Guidelines* 18/2 (Oxford: Bible Reading Fellowship, 2002), p. 102.
4. D. W. Winnicott, 'Ego distortion in terms of true and false self' in *The Maturational Processes and the Facilitating Environment* (London: Hogarth Press, 1982), p. 146.
5. Winnicott, 'Ego distortion', pp. 143, 150 and 152.
6. Leonard Shengold, *Soul Murder Revisited* (New Haven and London: Yale University Press, 1999), pp. 97, 101, 108.
7. Bruce Hopkins, 'Winnicott and the capacity to believe', *International Journal of Psycho-Analysis* 78/3 (1997), 492.
8. Henri J. M. Nouwen, *The Return of the Prodigal Son* (London: Darton, Longman & Todd, 1994), p. 52.
9. Nouwen, *The Return*, p. 53.
10. Nouwen, *The Return*, p. 53.

Chapter Seven: Returning home

1. Bonnie Thurston, 'Returning and rest 2' in *The Heart's Land* (Monmouthshire: Three Peaks Press, 2001).
2. George Orwell, *1984* (London: Penguin, 1989), p. 279.
3. Paul Tournier, *The Person Reborn* (London: SCM Press/Heinemann, 1967).
4. R. D. Hinshelwood, *Clinical Klein* (London: Free Association Books, 1994), p. 170.
5. Polly Young-Eisendrath, 'Psychotherapy as ordinary transcendence' in Polly Young-Eisendrath and Melvin E. Miller (eds), *The Psychology of Mature Spirituality* (London and New York: Routledge, 2000), p. 136.
6. Philip Larkin, 'Church Going' (28 July 1954) in *Collected Poems* (London and Boston: The Marvell Press and Faber & Faber, 1988), p. 98.
7. C. G. Jung, *Memories, Dreams, Reflections* (Glasgow: Fount, 1980), p. 356.
8. June Singer, *Modern Woman in Search of Soul* (York Beach, Maine: Nicolas-Hays, 1998), p. 43.
9. James Alison, 'The strangeness of passivity', talk for The Thomas Merton Society Conference (26 October 2002), pp. 3 and 9.
10. Henri J. M. Nouwen, *The Return of the Prodigal Son* (London: Darton, Longman & Todd, 1994), p. 105.

11. Richard Holloway, *Doubts and Loves* (Edinburgh: Canongate Books, 2001), p. 124.
12. Roberta Bondi, *Memories of God* (London: Darton, Longman & Todd, 1995). The extracts are taken from an earlier article by Bondi: 'Be not afraid: praying to God the Father', *Modern Theology* 9/3 (July 1993), 235–48, quotations from pp. 237–8, 239–40 and 245.
13. Thomas Merton, 'God' in William H. Shannon, Christine M. Bochen and Patrick F. O'Connell (eds), *The Thomas Merton Encyclopedia* (Maryknoll, NY: Orbis Books, 2002), pp. 182–3.
14. Martin Buber, *I and Thou* (Edinburgh: T. & T. Clark, 1970), pp. 78–80.
15. Thomas Merton, 'Eucharist', *The Thomas Merton Encyclopedia*, p. 142.

Chapter Eight: Held in love-scarred hands

1. Bonnie Thurston, 'Returning and rest 6' in *The Heart's Land* (Monmouthshire: Three Peaks Press, 2001).
2. George Lloyd Hodgkin in *Christian Faith and Practice in the Society of Friends* (London: London Yearly meeting of the Religious Society of Friends, 1960), quotation number 106.
3. D. W. Winnicott, 'Parent–infant relationship' in *The Maturational Processes and the Facilitating Environment* (London: Hogarth Press, 1982), pp. 44–6.
4. Adam Phillips, *Winnicott* (London: Fontana, 1988), p. 29.
5. Part of the collect for Wednesday midday prayer in *The Daily Office SSF* (London: Mowbray, 1992).
6. Paul Tillich, quoted in Richard Holloway, *Doubts and Loves* (Edinburgh: Canongate, 2001), p. 121.
7. Thomas Merton, *New Seeds of Contemplation* (London: Burns & Oates, 1999), p. 35.
8. Thomas Kelly, *A Testament of Devotion* (London: Hodder & Stoughton, 1961), p. 42.
9. Julian of Norwich, *Revelations of Divine Love* ch. 39 (long text), quoted by Gaynor Nurse in 'Harvesting our life: reflections on a spirituality of ageing', *Retreats* 181 (2002).
10. This is an expression used by Diana Francis in *People, Peace and Power* (London and Sterling, Va.: Pluto Press, 2002).
11. Thomas Merton, 'Resurrection' in *The Thomas Merton Encyclopedia*, ed. W. H. Shannon, C. M. Bochen and P. F. O'Connell (Maryknoll, NY: Orbis Books, 2002), p. 387.
12. This is part of a quotation from Shakespeare's *Macbeth*, which continues 'the grief that does not speak / Whispers the o'er fraught heart and bids it break' (*Macbeth* act 4, sc. 3, l. 209).
13. Rowan Williams, *Christ on Trial* (London: Fount, 2000), p. 126.
14. Rosemary Radford Ruether, 'God' in *Thomas Merton Encyclopedia*, p. 182. This phrase was used in a letter she wrote to Thomas Merton in February 1967.

15. Paul Tournier, *The Person Reborn* (London: SCM Press Ltd/Heinemann, 1967), pp. 29 and 31.
16. Thomas Merton, 'Contemplation' in *Thomas Merton Encyclopedia*, p. 83.
17. Brother Bernard, *Open to God* (London: Fount Paperbacks, 1986), p. 68.
18. Thomas Merton, 'The unconscious' in *Thomas Merton Encyclopedia*, p. 501.
19. Thomas Merton, 'Sacred Heart 2' in *The Collected Poems of Thomas Merton* (New York: New Directions, 1977).